PETERSON'S 1999

MBA
DISTANCE LEARNING PROGRAMS

The Hottest New Way to Earn a Graduate Business Degree

PETERSON'S
Princeton, New Jersey

About Peterson's

Peterson's is the country's largest educational information/communications company, providing the academic, consumer, and professional communities with books, software, and online services in support of lifelong education access and career choice. Well-known references include Peterson's annual guides to private schools, summer programs, colleges and universities, graduate and professional programs, financial aid, international study, adult learning, and career guidance. Peterson's Web site at petersons.com is the only comprehensive—and most heavily traveled—education resource on the Internet. The site carries all of Peterson's fully searchable major databases and includes financial aid sources, test-prep help, job postings, direct inquiry and application features, and specially created Virtual Campuses for every accredited academic institution and summer program in the U.S. and Canada that offers in-depth narratives, announcements, and multimedia features.

Visit Peterson's Education Center on the Internet (World Wide Web) at www.petersons.com

Editorial inquiries concerning this book should be addressed to the editor at: Peterson's, P.O. Box 2123, Princeton, New Jersey 08543-2123.

While every effort has been made to ensure the reliability of the information presented in this publication, the publisher does not guarantee the accuracy of the data contained herein. Inclusion of any institution or program does not imply an endorsement or judgment by the editors or publisher.

ISBN 0-7689-0125-1

Printed in the United States of America

10   9   8   7   6   5   4   3   2   1

Contents

How to Use This Book

What's Inside

This first edition of *MBA Distance Learning Programs* provides information to acquaint you with distance learning and with details on the institutions that offer it as an option for pursuing a master's-level business education.

Articles

To help you understand what is involved in pursuing a graduate business degree and what it is like to do so via distance education, there are articles to help you evaluate the value of graduate education, understand the advantages and disadvantages of learning from a distance, choose a program that is right for you, apply to programs electronically, pay for your education, and pursue opportunities after graduation and in the future.

Institution Profiles

Here you will find 100 institutions that offer graduate business education via distance learning. Profiles provide a general overview of each institution and the details you need to compare programs: course delivery sites, media, geographic and other restrictions, services, credit-earning options, application requirements, completion requirements, on-campus requirements, costs, registration, program

contact, degrees conferred, and individual course subjects.

In-Depth Descriptions

Additional details about distance learning offerings are provided by participating institutions in entries that describe unique aspects of their distance learning programs, including the special programs and services they offer and information about the faculty.

Finding What You Want

To help you make a decision about pursuing a graduate business degree via distance learning, you may want to read the articles first and then scan the profiles A to Z to get a sense of the requirements at different institutions. The comments from students in the article "What You Need to Know About Distance Learning" provide insight about what the day-to-day experience is really like.

Institution profiles are organized alphabetically by institution name to assist those students who are looking for a particular school. If you are interested in finding institutions in a particular state or another country, turn to the Geographic Index.

What's in the Profiles

Institution profiles appear in alphabetical order. The profile sections describe overall characteristics of an institution and details about its distance learning offerings.

Institutional Information

This section describes overall characteristics of an institution and its distance learning offerings.

General information: This section lists key facts and figures about the institution, including when it was founded, the type of accreditation it has, the number of students enrolled in graduate business distance learning, and the number of graduate business course titles offered at a distance.

Course delivery sites: This section lists the locations where distance learning students receive instruction—home, work, military bases, other colleges, off-campus centers, or other locations.

Media: This section describes the types of media used to deliver the courses and for student-teacher interaction. The following media are listed: television (broadcast or cable), videocassettes, videoconferencing (a two-way video connection via satellite, fiber optics, or other connection), interactive television, audiocassettes, audioconferencing (a two-way audio connection via telephone or other means), computer software, CD-ROM, computer conferencing, World Wide Web, e-mail, print, telephone, and fax. The lists of course delivery sites and media represent a summary of all options of all courses at the institution. Availability at particular sites and use of specific media vary from course to course; prospective students should contact the institution for details.

Geographic service area/ restrictions: This section outlines any geographical or other restrictions that may affect a student's eligibility to enroll in the institution's graduate business distance learning courses. Some of the institutions listed in the book serve only a local or in-state audience.

Services: This section lists the types of student services that are available at a distance through computer, phone, fax, or other means. These include library services, access to the campus computer network, e-mail services, tutoring, career-placement assistance, and academic advising.

Credit-earning options: This section lists alternative means of earning credit that are available to distance learning students at the institution. Among the possibilities are transfer from another institution, examinations, portfolio assessment, and military and business training programs.

Typical costs: This section lists the tuition and mandatory fees for distance learning courses and programs, based on 1997–98 figures. When costs differ based on where a student resides, the different figures for in-district, in-state, and out-of-state students are given. This section also indicates whether institutionally administered financial aid can be applied to courses or programs completed at a distance.

Registration: The following means of registering for courses are listed here: mail, fax, phone, e-mail, and World Wide Web.

Contact: This section lists the person or office to contact for more information about the institution's graduate business distance learning courses.

Graduate Degrees

This section lists the graduate-level business degree programs that the institution offers, how many students are enrolled in them, and how many degrees were earned in the most recent academic year.

Application requirements: This section lists what is required when applying to the program. This might include standardized test scores, college transcripts, letters of recommendation, and application fees.

Completion requirements: This section describes the specific courses required for the program, including the total number of credits or courses.

On-campus requirements: This section lists on-campus requirements, which may include brief orientations, weekend or weeklong seminars, or shorter residencies.

Individual Course Subjects

This section lists the subject areas in which the institution offers individual courses via distance learning.

How Institutions Get into the Book

To be included, all U.S. institutions must have full accreditation or candidate-for-accreditation (preaccreditation) status granted by an institutional or specialized accrediting body that is recognized by the U.S. Department of Education or the Council for Higher Education Accreditation. Canadian and other non-U.S. institutions must be chartered and authorized to grant degrees by the provincial or national government, affiliated with a chartered institution, or accredited by a recognized U.S. accrediting body.

Information in the Profiles and In-Depth Descriptions was collected in the spring and summer of 1998 through Peterson's Survey of Graduate Business Distance Learning Opportunities. Questionnaires were sent to more than 950 U.S. and international institutions that offer MBA and equivalent programs. Information was requested from program department contacts, admissions officers, or other appropriate personnel within these institutions in order to ensure its accuracy. In some cases, this information was supplemented with data that were available from school catalogs and brochures and, in some instances, directly from the institution's Web site on the Internet in order to provide as much detail as possible.

The omission of any particular item from a profile indicates that the item was either not applicable, not available at the time of publication, or not provided by the institution. Although Peterson's has every reason to believe that the information presented is accurate, students should check with each college and university to verify figures such as tuition and fees, which may have changed since the publication of this book.

Why an MBA? Future Trends and Opportunities in the Twenty-first Century

by John C. Hallenborg

MBA degrees are traditionally pursued in two-year, full-time programs; in more than two years in part-time evening and weekend programs; or in one-year intensive MBA programs, usually for executives or others with substantial work experience or those with undergraduate degrees in business.

Master's degrees of all types are on the rise. The plentiful supply of MBAs has allowed employers to be quite discriminating in hiring in recent years, requiring many MBAs to arrive equipped with specialized training and hands-on experience suited to their particular business niche.

In comparing the programs profiled in this volume, careful consideration should be given to the time required for studying, as every school varies in its expectations of students. At first, rather than merely communicating with targeted schools via letter, speak with someone in the admissions office who is familiar with your prospective course of study. Such a conversation will more than likely draw you closer to, or deter you from, participating in their program. Especially if you're holding down a job, it is always prudent to map out your time wisely.

Certainly, there are variations on this theme as the working MBA

Year	Master's Graduates in all Disciplines	Master's Graduates in Business and Management		
		Male	Female	Total
1990–91	337,168	50,883	27,372	78,255
1991–92	352,838	54,705	29,937	84,642
1992–93	369,585	57,651	31,964	89,615
1993–94	387,070	59,335	34,102	93,437
1994–95	397,629	59,109	34,700	93,809

Source: National Center for Education Statistics, U.S. Department of Education. Figures were unavailable beyond 1995.

candidate may, for example, distribute a course load to accommodate a work schedule. There is also the related issue of employer assistance. The candidate's choice of school or program might be determined solely by which programs are endorsed and subsidized by the candidate's employer.

The one-year program has been around long enough for employers to gauge many of its attributes as compared to the two-year counterpart. One consensus is that there are many other issues that are more likely to clearly differentiate one candidate from another. An MBA degree can improve a candidate's chances to approximately the same level as a non-MBA candidate with more years of successful work experience.

Of course, the weight assigned to the MBA degree by prospective employers varies considerably, depending on the industry, company, and job assignment. For the savvy salesperson of copiers at a large firm such as Xerox, for example, the company's in-house training would provide more valuable background than an MBA degree, at least until a promotion incorporated management skills into the position. Conversely, someone applying for a middle-management job in the finance department at a mid-size company may find an MBA degree indispensable. The point is, the two jobs might be represented on the same salary tier, so it is still a maxim in the transitional process from MBA school to the workplace that the degree's importance is job-specific.

There are other key intangibles that have significance. Acquiring an advanced degree may imbue certain candidates with a feeling of confidence that may signal the difference between a lackluster career wandering the halls of a nondescript organization and a robust, life-affirming career full of welcome challenges and even more welcome rewards.

The knowledge gained in acquiring the MBA degree is not to be taken for granted at any point in the hiring process, as MBA holders can expect dedicated human resource executives to grill potential new hires in detail as to their educational experiences. What can the MBA grad do to improve this process? Graduates can apply their newly acquired knowledge to specific corporate examples to show why they should be hired.

Closing the Loop: Business Schools and Corporations

Ambitious MBA candidates in the late 1990s, looking forward to their careers or perhaps to the exciting prospect of entrepreneurship, cannot afford to presume that every MBA program will meet the educational requirements specific to an industry or profession. In today's job market and that of the near future, the MBA graduate will be expected to deliver both technical and nontechnical skills in every business and industrial sector. As in other areas of graduate study and related employment, the focus is, and will continue to be, on specialized expertise in business management. For business, opportunities abound to work with universities to create new MBA programs that will prepare candidates to fulfill an array of specialized leadership roles. For schools, this phenomenon continues to spur revamping of curricula almost annually to keep pace with the real-world demands that will be placed upon future MBA graduates.

Is it safe to presume that the recruitment managers at most major companies are aware of the changing makeup of the leading business school programs? The answer is most definitely yes and apparent in the variety of degree options, concentrations, and alternative courses of study available to today's MBA student.

How the degree can be obtained today also closely mirrors current business trends—the expectation of an early return on investment, preferably within one to two years. Future MBA programs will likely continue to reflect the choices seen today: the one-year degree, which often dispenses with core programs in favor of specialized courses tailored to specific career paths, and the more traditional two-year and extended MBA programs, which have been the basis of graduate business degrees for decades.

Certainly for the last twenty years or so, benchmark companies and top graduate schools have worked intensively to match academic programs to corporate needs. These relationships are likely to strengthen as more corporations and prospective students, hesitant to invest in two-year programs, are more willing to commit to emerging one-year programs.

Two-Year MBA vs. One-Year MBA

By all accounts, the composition of the MBA degree and how it is acquired will change significantly over the next five to ten years. The perceived value of the MBA degree has changed considerably in the student community and within the corporations that hire MBA graduates by the thousands every year. After a period of flat growth several years ago, the degree now appears dynamic and evolving. Affordable, highly focused, and time-efficient versions of the degree have replaced some multiyear courses of study.

The upsurge seen recently in one-year degrees has been driven, for the most part, by corporate demand, serving mostly experienced professionals and recent undergraduates with some work experience. Although two-year programs are still the norm in most business schools, accelerated and specialized one-year programs are seeing slight increases in enrollment. Business schools have been adversely affected by this trend and are offering degree options that combine an undergraduate business degree with an MBA in a five-year program.

The primary difference between one-year and traditional two-year programs is that with the shorter version, there is little if any overlap with undergraduate business curricula. Thus, it is highly recommended that students who decide on a one-year program enroll soon after receiving their undergraduate degrees and be able to satisfy all core business course requirements. However, some

Steven Lavender, President, Morgan/Webber: retained search firm

In answering the one-year versus two-year MBA program question, I have high regard for both programs at top schools such as Harvard, Wharton, Boston University, MIT's Sloan, Stanford, and the University of Chicago.

In the intensive one-year program, the student really lives the program in that time frame. I see it as a firm plus on a resume. A two-year program offers an assignment-oriented course of study, as the student has more time to assert his or her ideas as an individual versus the largely company-oriented slant of one-year programs.

Both of these programs add an attractive package of improved skills to the corporate world, reflecting course study in planning; distribution; the modern structure of marketing; assessments of MIS requirements; and the practical implementation of useful business models.

Right now, I don't have any clients who request an MBA. Work experience is still preferred as background for most positions. The MBA is still making a comeback as a hiring asset.

My searches today indicate that the person with a very general background—with a liberal arts BA and an MBA in management—might command $4000 more in salary than the BA-only candidate, on average—not much considering what acquiring the degree might have cost.

If you are considering an MBA, gear the course work toward a specialization and limit your choice of schools to those that include the targeted curriculum. This way, you will bring a continued focus on a specialty that today's employers find attractive.

You may wonder when, in a career, it's a good time to acquire an MBA. In today's job market, it's best if you work for six or seven years and then go get yourself an MBA. By the time someone has six years' work experience, he or she knows enough to properly shape a course of MBA study that will be beneficial to the employer.

---

one-year programs require from two to five years' work experience in lieu of the traditional first-year MBA core study courses. In most cases, one-year elective courses are all but tailored to the applicant's career, so that the graduate can reenter the workforce as quickly as possible. Classic two-year programs most often focus on elective and specialized course work in the second year after completion of core requirements in the first year.

A number of emerging realities will highlight the one-year MBA degree: technology-based information media will replace class time in many cases as students gain access to CD-ROM and online services; fewer faculty members may be required as schools combine resources to teach fewer classes to more students; and distance learning will replace some on-campus classes. For most schools and students of the future, technology will certainly dictate the learning medium.

In the relatively brief period that one-year MBA graduates have been working, corporations have been neutral about recruiting one-year program versus two-year program graduates, as there is no published evidence that graduates of two-year programs outperform their one-year counterparts.

Albert W. Niemi Jr., Dean of Southern Methodist University's Edwin L. Cox School of Business, explains that "I don't see, in the data that we have collected—in terms of starting salaries—that there is any difference in the way one-year people are treated by industry. One-year grads do as well as two-year grads in terms of earning power in the marketplace."

Despite Niemi's findings, to date there has not been significant movement toward the one-year degree, as at present there are relatively few such programs compared to the total number of MBA programs offered nationwide.

Traditional Course Work vs. In-house Training

Rather than sending employees off company premises for continuing education, many companies may choose to hire competent teachers as staff members to provide in-house training. This trend is not yet fully under way, but it is seen as a cost-effective alternative to traditional MBA programs. The one-year MBA and in-house training represent new models for graduate education. "Our dynamic economy is forcing change on all of us, if we are to be competitive and meet new challenges," offers William K. Laidlaw Jr., Executive Vice President of AACSB–The International Association for Management Education.

Among the programs on the horizon are those directed at problem solving within a limited number of companies or even a single company. These programs are tailored to specific company issues. Typically, collaborative tutoring teams are composed of university professors and corporate upper management.

Changes in the Financial Sector

In the top tiers of the financial markets, there have been many changes following the scandals and management excesses of the 1980s. By close association with these events, the reputation of the MBA degree was somewhat tainted, directly or by implication. Today's graduates are under scrutiny to improve the standing of the degree in the academic and corporate worlds. Clearly, teamwork has superseded personal glory in most corporate environments, and the financial community is no exception.

There has been a considerable shakeout in the better sectors of the financial job market, and many large financial organizations are as vigilant in maintaining a positive

L. Nicholas Deane, former Senior Vice President, Faulkner & Gray, subsidiary of Thomson Financial Services

Faulkner & Gray is a departmentalized organization, and as head of a division that publishes content for professionals in the tax field, I tend to value work experience in that particular area more than a general MBA degree. However, I do recognize the usefulness of MBAs that target disciplines more specifically than, for example, an MBA in marketing, which I do not value very highly. However, in considering my department's needs, I'll flag a resume with an MBA with taxation as a specialty.

My sense is that work experience has more value than an MBA in general business environments, but that as one swings toward the more technical domains, a technically based MBA will look more attractive to an employer. The likelihood is that such a candidate will get up to speed more quickly on what is happening, both good and bad, within a company. And then, there is a greater chance that background in the specific area will serve to provide a base for successful decision making.

The in-depth study of sophisticated financial concepts is the key attribute that sets the MBA degree apart. I like to see well-placed employees armed with this advanced knowledge of finance. All sharp-minded candidates deserve a fair shot. There are experienced people who perform well without an MBA degree. Faulkner & Gray is typical of the high end of the publishing sector that is using technology to migrate from paper-based products to online and other electronically based formats.

As to the one-year degree versus the two-year degree, I have not seen evidence that causes me to prefer a two-year degree over the one-year alternative, but I should stress again that pertinent work background has been a better indicator of good hires than degrees of any sort. It comes down to the individual, really, the candidate's unique mix of experiences and qualifications. One area that I have seen strength in as the MBA relates to job specs is in financial analysis. I have come to expect the MBA holder to be sophisticated in crunching numbers.

public image as they are about profit levels. Any MBA candidate seeking a spot at one of the top investment banks, for example, will have to be aware of issues of public relations in addition to more predictable questions about money markets. Expect this sensitivity to public opinion to remain high for many years. In fact, a reputation for aboveboard dealings is nearly as important as bottom-line performance in today's financial sphere.

At present, the MBA degree is still key in the world of investment banking, as recruitment specialists at banks large and small report that about 90 percent of new hires have the degree.

The New MBA Attitude

How does this job market realignment affect the MBA holder's chances for a lucrative career in finance? The answer is often more in the attitude of the prospect than in the present and future states of the job market. These behavioral issues resound throughout not only the financial sector but also the finance departments of major corporations. The message is: bring us good grades from a good school but also bring along maturity and a problem-solving attitude.

Despite the fact that compensation at the higher levels in banking is very bonus-oriented, the fresh MBA graduate should avoid being a self-serving maverick. The MBA of tomorrow, more than ever before, will have to display strengths in leadership, teamwork, problem solving, and dealing with people. Upper management will be looking for well-rounded individuals who offer a balanced perspective and are ready and able to apply their education in a real-life setting.

Working for Smaller Companies

And what about the option of employment by the thousands of small and mid-size firms that populate the American business landscape? The ideal of a "secure job forever" has been replaced by the reality that most Americans will have two or three careers in their lifetimes and may even change jobs every five years or so. Small and middle-market corporations have become the most fertile ground for MBA recruit-

ment in the 1990s and will likely continue to hire more MBAs into the next century. In many instances, it is easier for a talented MBA holder to make a significant contribution to a mid-size firm in a high-growth mode. The key, of course, may be to identify likely high-growth companies that have the potential for continued growth over a three- to five-year period.

Once again, preparation for a specific industry niche, or better yet a specific company or companies, is key to landing those choice spots that feature a daunting 50:1, or 500:1, applicant/position ratio. Most competing MBAs are aware that the key to landing the desired job is to positively differentiate oneself from other equally qualified candidates. Some MBA students have gone so far as to research potential employers at the beginning of their course work, studying the details of annual reports, product brochures, etc., for the duration of the typical two-year MBA program.

Skills learned in MBA core and specialized courses can be especially valuable in helping to transform technical ideas and concepts into tangible, marketable products. In both large and small businesses in the future, managers will certainly be expected to bring not only technical expertise to the table but also the ability to translate new ideas into profit-sustaining products and services.

The small and mid-size firm is often the perfect venue for such creative expression coupled with pragmatic implementation. Smaller firms are already actively recruiting

Bril Flint, former Vice President, Strategic Planning, EMI-Capital Music

When recruiting management talent for my team, I evaluate candidates across four dimensions: the candidate's long-term career plan and objectives; relevant real-world experience; technical capabilities for the job at hand; and interpersonal skills.

With these parameters in mind, how can a prospective business school student make the best use of an MBA education within the context of overall career advancement?

First, make sure graduate management education really does fit in with your long-term career plan. This may sound like a trivial step, but I have met more people that have not explicitly delineated their objectives than those that have. You can change them as you go along, but make sure the time and money you will spend on business school are really worthwhile.

I also like to see candidates who factor their long-term strategy into their choice of business school. For example, if they want to pursue a career in engineering management, did they pick a school that has a good program in that field, or did they opt for a "name school to get their ticket punched?" I prefer to see the former.

While an MBA from a top school can be a leg up on the competing candidates, I have seen enough successful executives with degrees from middle or lower tier graduate management programs (and many without an MBA degree at all) to know that a degree from a top ten institution is not required to prove and validate the individual's capability. Neither is it a guarantee of success, as I have seen plenty of graduates from top tier schools fail miserably in the working world.

Relevant work experience is really the most important area for me when I look at recruits. Most executives would rather have someone who understands their industry and how it works. I usually prefer the candidate with two years of relevant industry experience over one with two years of business school, no matter how "applied" a business school curriculum claims to be. It simply cannot duplicate the real day-to-day business activity in a particular industry or company.

The bottom line here is: It is better to work several years before you go to business school. (*Editor's Note:* Flint has a master's degree in management from MIT's Sloan School of Management.) If you have identified an industry in which you really want to work long term, go all out to find a job in that line of business before you go to business school. This may mean sacrificing short-term earnings.

(continued)

I look for candidates who can bring the right "tool box" to the job for which I am recruiting. The appropriate technical skills for the position under consideration can be developed and demonstrated through prior experience, whether in the same industry or in the same functional area in a different line of business.

To a lesser, but still important, extent, specific technical skills can be learned in school. To reiterate, if your long-term career strategy should help drive your choice of business school, then developing the appropriate technical capabilities should be the tactical driver in your selection of specific courses to take. In the typical two-year business school program, you have a limited number of elective courses. Make each one count to your advantage; try to leave business school with the appropriate tools at your disposal.

Interpersonal skills have a profound impact on a manager's long-term career path. In every meeting or transaction, others are making assessments of your poise, level of confidence, ability to communicate clearly, your business ethics, competency, and about one hundred other interpersonal traits. As in the other areas, prior work experience is most valuable in developing this skill set. Watch how successful executives interact in a variety of business settings.

Business school is also a good setting to enhance your interpersonal abilities. Working and socializing with classmates from varied backgrounds is good experience and is essential to get the most out of the business school experience.

from the ranks of new MBA degree holders to discover the talented individuals whose skills and judgment will drive future growth and product improvement.

MBA candidates should be very selective in targeting small and mid-size companies, however, as many smaller firms are adopting a lean corporate structure by not instituting a middle layer of management until they reach the 1,000-employee mark. For the MBA holder this may mean more responsibility within a flat organizational structure and the need to "wear many hats." High-tech, high-growth, small to mid-size firms such as Dallas Semiconductor (Dallas, TX) with 1,350 employees; software maker Wonderware (Irvine, CA), with 425 employees; and

California Micro Devices (Milpitas, CA) with 260 employees are all focused on hiring individuals with variations of the master's degree.

Richard Helfrich, former Vice President at California Micro, a semiconductor maker, considers the MBA to be "a strong plus in our hiring considerations. I weigh the degree as the equivalent of three years of solid work experience. But because our products are so technology-based, the master's degree is still our primary qualifier."

Tomorrow's MBA Entrepreneur

There will also be a place for the ambitious MBA holder who cannot wait for others to bring his or her ideas to the marketplace. For many fearless graduates, starting or buying a business may be a quicker and more lucrative route to success. Those with the best chance of making it this way will most likely combine prior technical training with the marketing and financial knowledge acquired with an MBA degree—for example, the electrical engineering whiz who starts a small, niche-focused circuit design firm.

Still, the appeal of running a small business does not get as much media coverage as it should, if the Harvard MBA Class of 1970 is any indication. In a recent survey of the 723 alumni who are now as a group generally in the peak phases of their careers, only 13 percent worked for *BusinessWeek* 1000 companies. By contrast, 36 percent were self-employed and the majority worked in small businesses (fewer than 500 employees) in one capacity or another.

Opportunities for MBAs in the Year 2000

Because management and finance are functions common to every conceivable type of business or industry, it is difficult to make predictions about job growth for MBAs in particular markets. However, although it may sound simplistic, it is still true that career opportunities will most likely continue to exist for talented MBAs in nearly all areas of the marketplace into the next century. Although manufacturing and investment firms have experienced somewhat of a downswing in top management positions in the last few

years, a tremendous variety of positions still attract MBAs to accounting, commercial banking, management consulting, consumer products, health care, insurance, services, and chemical companies in functions that include marketing, finance, operations, information systems, and long-term planning. Even many nonprofits are recruiting MBAs to help them redefine and reshape their organizations both economically and socially.

So, what are some of the growth areas for the MBA graduates to consider? As in the 1980s and early 1990s, there appears to be no limit to the growth potential in the software and telecommunications industries, particularly in the convergence of data and voice technologies. The number of professional jobs in computer software and hardware development and marketing will also likely only increase over the next ten years, although many companies may start up and then fold or be bought out in these volatile fields.

Telecommunications giants such as AT&T, MCI, and the Regional Bell Companies are already driving much of the development in this sector and will certainly require MBA graduates with a broad range of business and technical skills. MBAs with well-honed analytical and marketing skills will certainly be needed as telecommunications companies continue making forays into the information and entertainment services markets.

Another area for consideration by the eager MBA is publishing and information services. Innumerable products in CD-ROM, CD-I, and online formats are displacing paper equivalents most notably in the professional and academic domains. Books, newspapers, and other information products are certain to follow this trend toward electronic versus paper distribution. Publishing professionals armed with MBA degrees will certainly supply much of the marketing, financial, and strategic expertise needed to help such companies enter these new markets.

Still another high-growth area that may lure many MBAs is the world of entertainment. The creative entrepreneur seeking entry into the television, film, or music industry could be well positioned with an MBA, since bottom-line business issues usually determine if projects are produced. Consulting opportunities for the freelance MBA holder are already numerous in the entertainment industry. This should continue as a promising area of activity for the creative MBA.

For U.S.–based firms in other industry sectors, a significant amount of future growth may come from overseas operations. In the chemicals and polymers sector, for example, many of the management jobs will be in maintaining investments on the Pacific Rim and Eastern Europe, where most of the largest petrochemical conglomerates have joint ventures in place. MBA graduates should be willing to travel abroad to land these types of positions.

Most sources indicate that U.S. industries overall will experience moderate, 3 to 7 percent annual growth in the next ten years. Hiring of MBAs in industries such as construction and real estate, general manufacturing, foods and beverages, and electronics is predicted to be moderate by comparison.

Which sectors will be the toughest to enter, based on a flat industry growth forecast for the next ten years? Aerospace, oil and gas, health care, retail, and apparel are some of the major industries that are likely to experience fluctuating growth at best.

Go Global

By the year 2000, with the continued advance of telecommunications as the primary medium for data transfer, banks and corporations will have permanently erased many commercial barriers between nations. This borderless, global market should be an exciting prospect for the ambitious MBA.

An in-depth review of international trade regulations will serve tomorrow's MBA well since American firms already derive some 50 percent of gross revenues from overseas operations. Given the prodigious growth rate of economies in the developing nations, particularly in Asia and South America, virtually any MBA with skills to lend to those markets should find much success.

There will be more exciting opportunities in the former Eastern Bloc nations as these countries struggle to establish free-market economies. But the challenges are as enormous as the potential rewards. Still, the fearless MBA, armed with street smarts, a good command of the host country's language, and a firm grasp

Willard Anderson, former Director, Management Development and Diversity, ITT Corporation

At ITT, the MBA degree is very important as part of an overall package of attributes a candidate may have to offer. When we hire an MBA, we expect that new hire to hit the ground running, as there is less time in today's competitive marketplace for in-house training.

We presume that an MBA holder emerging from our group of recruitment schools (Harvard, Columbia, Duke, Northwestern, Wharton, and Stanford) will have considerable business acumen. This is part of the skill set we are seeking. Another key element is an undergraduate course of study that integrates well with the curriculum that was chosen in acquiring an MBA.

Also important in terms of middle-management jobs and marketing leadership positions is that the candidate have three to five years' solid work experience. So, we look for people who have a synergistic mix of MBA and relevant undergraduate training, along with some real time spent solving real business problems.

As to the question of one-year versus two-year MBA programs, we are decidedly in favor of two-year programs. In fact, exceptions are very few. Perhaps 1 in 100 MBA holders will come on board with a one-year degree. This conservative approach has paid off in that we have reaped significant rewards from this hiring system.

We also view the MBA degree as more important today than it was five or ten years ago. In order to move easily within the extensive ITT corporate system, a new management employee needs to be familiar with sophisticated business models and other more advanced business concepts that reflect exposure to the rigors of acquiring an MBA degree. Our undergraduate employees are more deterministic in how they go about their jobs. MBA holders are much more likely to get into developmental work right away.

Overall, ITT is a company that all but requires management candidates to have a two-year MBA and three to five years of work experience. In terms of specialties within the MBA degree, we have had notable success with candidates who stressed finance and marketing in their courses of study.

---

of the cultural keys to market entry, will find plenty of qualified European partners ready to forge ahead.

Similarly, at home, most large companies will be importing and exporting huge quantities of commodities, consumer goods, and financial services. For American MBAs seeking careers at home, the importance of global awareness cannot be overstated. Ten years from now, there will be impressive opportunities for international licensing of technologies, trademarks, and copyrighted products and processes that most Americans take for granted. Clearly, the cosmopolitan MBA will be the first to reap the rewards from emerging international markets in the twenty-first century.

Postgrad Tips

A candidate should zero in on three to five companies that are very attractive, firms wherein one could happily spend the next three to ten years working hard to establish oneself in the business community. If writing is a strong skill, parlay the skill by writing a detailed letter expressing your knowledge of the industry and the company and why you would be an asset to that company.

In the case of public companies, get their latest annual report, analyze it, and have your own views on the company's future ready to share with your interviewer. Do not make the mistake of blindly agreeing with everything the interviewer offers about the firm. If you disagree on a point, assert yourself with an explanation of your perspective on the issue. Never shy away from creating polarized discussion during an interview if you truly believe your position to be correct. Hopefully, your interviewer will recognize your willingness to defend your viewpoint as a trait of a successful executive.

John C. Hallenborg is a writer and business consultant based in Los Angeles, California.

The New MBA: What to Look for in Today's Reinvented Programs

by Carter A. Prescott

Your team's assignment: Climb through different size openings in a massive rope web without touching anything—and do it faster than competing teams. Another assignment: Tell a fellow student about an experience in which you felt odd or left out. Sound like typical MBA fare? If you answered yes, you pass.

Today's graduate business programs are undergoing what some experts tout as nothing less than revolutionary change. In response to new competitive demands on corporations and increasing globalization—both of which require tomorrow's business leaders to be flexible and manage workforces and internal structures that cross cultural and political lines—MBA programs are diversifying and redefining themselves. You'll still graduate with a firm grounding in the staples of business education—finance, strategy, operations management, marketing, and the like—but you'll also learn how to work in teams, how to motivate others, and how to see the "big picture" when solving problems. Strong communication and interpersonal skills are just as important in today's new MBA programs as technical knowledge and the ability to "crunch numbers."

"There's more churning going on right now in management education than at any time in thirty-five years," says Charles W. Hickman, Director of Projects and Services at AACSB–The International Association for Management Education, which accredits MBA programs in the United States. "The emphasis today is changing from teaching to learning," Hickman notes. "The front-end-load module, where you dump two years of education into a student's head and then sew it up, is over. The world is moving too fast. Companies want MBA graduates to know how to learn, because lifelong learning is the key to success for practicing managers and executives. The MBA is not an end in itself. It positions the degree-holder for a variety of general management positions."

What, you may ask, can you expect to learn from the rope exercise? How to plan, pay attention to detail, and how to work in teams. And the lesson behind baring your soul to a colleague? How to become sensitive to gender and ethnic diversity in order to manage it effectively.

The days when MBA graduates could dazzle their bosses with only a few mentions of decision trees, regression analysis, net present value, and gap planning are gone. You'll still learn these concepts, but you'll be synthesizing them into a broader skill set. Dennis J. Weidenaar, Dean of the Krannert Graduate School of Management at Purdue University, calls it the "new management environment." He says it is characterized by "teamwork and alliances, continuous changes in technologies, globalization, and networks that are in instantaneous communication with each other."

How specifically do today's MBA programs prepare you to succeed in this environment? Here are ten primary ways.

1. Cross-Functional, Interdisciplinary Curricula

You'll hear these phrases so often they'll sound like a mantra. Even the venerable Harvard Business School voted to overhaul its MBA curriculum, effective in 1996, to offer students more interdisciplinary courses and more freedom in choosing electives. Across the country, MBA schools are reshaping curricula to teach students the importance of solving problems by synthesizing a variety of subjects. Faculty members from different disciplines coordinate their syllabi and teach in teams to students who work in teams. When Stanford added a new course in human resource management, for example, it was

designed by professors of organizational behavior and economics. A cross-functional approach also has proved resoundingly popular with students. After Wharton tested a dramatically revised curriculum, surveys showed that a full 94 percent of its 1993 graduates who participated in the pilot would do so again, while 60 percent of those who studied under the traditional program would have preferred the new one.

2. New Programs

Whether they are specific sequences or subjects woven into the fabric of an MBA curriculum, you'll find strong mentions of entrepreneurship, ethics, Total Quality Management (TQM), information technology management, and leadership development in nearly all basic MBA programs. Purdue's PL+S Program (Preparing Leaders and Stewards) provides additional course work, community service opportunities, self-assessment, and self-directed team consulting projects with companies, all as avenues for developing leadership skills. Harvard's new "foundations" program will place heavy emphasis on career planning, self-assessment, working in groups, and business ethics. Ethical challenges are constantly reinforced in the Pepperdine University curriculum, says Stanley K. Mann, a professor in the Graduate School of Business. "We are training managers to take on responsibilities and obligations, not to put the dollar ahead of everything else."

A new emphasis on entrepreneurship reflects the reality that "the majority of MBA graduates will not work in Fortune 500 companies, because they have been downsizing the most," notes Charles Hickman of the AACSB. Accordingly, many universities help students develop better job-hunting and career development skills.

3. Global Perspectives

Because U.S. corporations increasingly compete around the world, globalization is serious business in the nation's MBA programs. Stanford offers four times as many internationally focused electives as it did ten years ago. Even though Pace University has featured an international business major for twenty years, "we now view it as a jumping-off point to integrate international issues throughout the curriculum," says Associate Dean Arthur L. Centonze. Pepperdine University in Malibu, California, designed a specific Master of International Business program that features eight months of study and internships in France or Germany. Students are required to find their own internships and to be proficient in French or German. Although 6 percent routinely drop out, another third stay abroad for at least a year, postponing their graduation to gain valuable work experience.

4. Increased Student and Faculty Diversity

Business schools have realized that the best way to teach tomorrow's managers to tap the talents of an increasingly diverse workforce is to surround students with a widely diverse student body. They're also recruiting more faculty members who reflect diverse viewpoints and philosophies as well as national origin. While more and more schools are quick to point to their rising numbers of international students, they also refer to the diverse backgrounds and experiences among their MBA students. Students from diverse countries and backgrounds are viewed as a resource that complements what faculty members know and what other students bring to the program. Women students are swelling the ranks of MBA graduates as well.

5. Teamwork, Teamwork, and More Teamwork

Schools are working hard to encourage the same environment of teamwork that graduates will experience in the working world. "Cohort structures," for example, have gained in popularity. Cohorts means that you are placed with a specified number of fellow students— deliberately chosen for their diversity—either for the first few weeks of class or for the entire first year. Together with other members of your cohort, you'll solve problems as a team, resolve conflicts, sustain morale, achieve accountability, and, it is hoped, learn to reach your goals by becoming interdependent, just as you would in a corporate setting.

Reinvented MBA programs are learning to "pit students against the curriculum and not against one another," says Sam Lundquist, Chief of Staff in the Dean's Office at

Wharton. Stanford says its cooperative learning environment is a significant factor in the program's "joy coefficient," as George Parker, Associate Dean for Academic Affairs, describes it.

6. Richer Learning Environment

Hand in hand with curriculum improvements, business schools are finding new ways to strengthen teaching and foster improved student-faculty relationships. Indeed, the "most exciting part" of Wharton's new cross-functional curriculum, Lundquist says, is that teams of faculty now teach the same students for the entire first year, which "drastically improves the quality of relationships between students and faculty members."

As MBA programs bolster the quality of the learning experience, they are focusing a laser beam on how well professors help students learn. Pace University views faculty members as "the managers of the student learning process," says Centonze. As a result, all programs and courses have objectives that are measured by student exit surveys, faculty questionnaires, and yearly performance evaluations for faculty members. Any underperforming teachers are coached at the school's Center for Faculty Development and Teaching Effectiveness, where their syllabi are reviewed and their classes videotaped.

Increasingly, a variety of teaching methods are employed, including lectures, case studies, computer simulations, and consulting projects.

Harvard's curriculum reform was notable for adopting alternative teaching methods in addition to its reliance on the traditional case-study approach and for developing ways to have faculty members spend less time teaching basics.

7. Greater Use of Learning Technologies

MBA programs are making increasing use of such state-of-the-art technologies as distance learning, which uses interactive cable television and computers to take courses directly to students' homes. The University of Maryland, for instance, uses distance learning and team teaching to bundle its assets and hire big-name teachers. Distance learning also is "favored heavily" in Europe, where virtually all programs are part-time, according to Roger McCormick, director general of the Association of MBA's in the United Kingdom. Distance learning allows students to learn at their own pace, which is especially helpful for remedial courses and quantitative work, he says.

Business schools are avidly employing other technologies as well, such as interactive cases on CD and real-time data feeds from Wall Street. In fall 1996, the University of Texas at Austin completed a $1.5-million trading room so that its students could experience trading in real time with real dollars from a $2-million investment fund. Purdue is even investigating how to bring virtual reality experiences into the classroom. Meanwhile, videoconferencing is used for classroom presentations or off-site interviews with corporations.

8. More Applied Learning

At the University of Illinois at Chicago, student and faculty teams tackle corporate projects by interviewing corporate executives, writing reports, and presenting recommendations to the company and to their fellow students. They're not alone. Students at the University of Texas at Austin helped Ford Motor Company better segment its Hispanic marketing efforts. The University of Michigan adopted a medical school model, requiring students to get considerable practical experience working at corporations. At Stanford, corporate leaders such as Andrew S. Grove of Intel team with professors to teach classes on strategy in the high-technology industry.

9. Strategic Alliances

To better leverage their resources, schools are joining forces to teach students and to conduct postgraduate training for corporate executives. The Thunderbird School reserves seats at its learning centers around the world for its partner schools in the United States. Business schools at the University of Florida and Fordham University in New York team up with AT&T and MCI, respectively, to offer customized programs for their executives. Corporate advisory boards, long a staple of most MBA programs, are increasingly relied on to provide advice on curricula as well as hiring opportunities. Corporate partners

also contribute other sorely needed resources. Purdue has one of the most extensive computing labs of any business school, thanks to the generosity of such high-tech partners as AT&T, Hewlett Packard, IBM, Microsoft, and PictureTel. "The business environment is moving fast, and even elite schools don't have all the money they need to access new markets, technology, and faculty expertise," says the AACSB's Hickman.

10. Customer Focus

It's not uncommon to hear business school professors routinely refer to students and companies as customers—and to treat their needs with the same respect. Many schools are applying Total Quality Management (TQM) principles to operating the business schools themselves. They're becoming more customer-focused, reducing the cycle time for admissions processing and curriculum development, and becoming more efficient to lower tuition or keep it from rising quickly. Seattle University takes classes to the customers, dispatching faculty members to teach evening and breakfast courses near Seattle's biggest employers.

With such evolution occurring day by day at business schools, more than ever before, today's reinvented MBA programs aim to prepare you for the real world of work, where you will work in teams, take a global view, and analyze problems from a multitude of perspectives. To accomplish these goals, MBA programs intend to equip you with the ability to embrace change, accept ambiguity, and lead others with the vision and confidence gained from continuous learning.

With a newly minted MBA degree, you are better qualified to enter new fields, better able to leverage your prior work experience, and more likely to sustain higher earnings over the course of your career. Equally important, you'll have the opportunity to make a significant difference on as broad a scale as you wish. With finely honed analytical skills, the ability to work well with people, and the desire to keep learning, today's MBA graduates can succeed in a broad range of general management positions and add more value than ever before.

———————

Carter A. Prescott is a management communications consultant in New York City.

Getting Admitted to MBA Programs

by Samuel T. Lundquist, Chief of Staff, Dean's Office, The Wharton School, University of Pennsylvania

Applicants to MBA programs often spend more time trying to figure out how to get into business school than researching the program itself. Hence, the prospective student has made the first critical error of the admissions process—seeking the elusive "admissions formula" versus making a quality presentation that demonstrates knowledge of self and graduate business education.

There really is not any formula that can predict admission to an MBA program. Business school applicants must enter the selection process understanding the difference between being admissible and being admitted. The distinction between the two varies considerably among business schools, depending on the level of selectivity in the admissions process. While some MBA programs admit all qualified students, others may deny admission to 4 of every 5 applicants who are qualified to be admitted. Understanding this difference is the first step to a successful application.

The Evaluative Process

Applicants to MBA programs should understand how they will be evaluated during the admissions process. In general, presentation, academic profile, professional work experience, and personal qualities will be the four areas in which each applicant will be evaluated. Admissions officers generally evaluate the factors influencing applicants' educational and professional decisions and the corresponding outcomes. Admissions committees do not spend a lot of time evaluating the labels that tend to categorize applicants into special groups. For instance, candidates for admission often assume that the quality of the undergraduate institution that they attended will affect the outcome of their application. A common misconception is that applicants with undergraduate degrees from Ivy League schools are always more desirable candidates for business schools. In fact, the undergraduate institution one attended may not be a significant variable in the admissions process at some business schools.

Applicants are evaluated as individuals. The environment in which they have studied or worked is relevant only when it is given meaning in the context of their life experiences. How the culture of a campus or workplace has influenced one's success is interesting and important to the admissions committee's ability to fully evaluate an application. Therefore, applicants who provide only factual information about their academic and professional profile miss the opportunity to present the most compelling and distinguishing characteristics of their candidacy.

The MBA degree is not a professional license that is required to practice management. Therefore, people of all ages are known to pursue the degree. Older applicants (32 years old and up) often fear that because they are atypical to the traditional graduate school student profile they will be less desirable to business schools. On the contrary, older students offer professional experience, maturity, and perspective that are highly valued in the classroom. The admissions committee does expect older applicants to have highly developed reasons for pursuing the MBA at this stage of their lives. Post-MBA goals are expected to be clearer and more defined than those of their younger counterparts.

Applicants have much more control of the admissions process than they realize. Prospective students determine all of the information that is presented in the application forms, essays, and interviews. They even get to select the people who will serve as references to support their candidacy. The only aspect of the process that an applicant does not control is the competition; that is, who else applies for admission. It is the competition

that will determine the threshold between admissibility and acceptance.

Presentation is obviously one of the most important factors in admission. Four other areas are evaluated during the evaluative process. They include academic profile, GMAT score, professional work experience, and personal qualities.

Academic Profile

Business schools seek students who can survive the demands of a rigorous program, and the best way to show your intellectual strength is to demonstrate strong classroom achievement and high aptitude. Your ability to excel as an undergraduate student is directly related to your ability to succeed in a graduate program.

Your undergraduate specialization will have little effect on admission to business school. It is not necessary to take undergraduate courses in business administration because most MBA programs offer or require a core curriculum of basic business courses as part of the graduate degree. However, it is advisable to have basic skills in economics, calculus, and statistics in preparation for graduate study in business.

The Graduate Management Admission Test (GMAT)

Most business schools require applicants to submit the results of their Graduate Management Admission Test (GMAT). The importance of the GMAT in admissions will vary depending on the school. Minimum score requirements do not exist at some business schools. Test scores are certainly not the sole criterion for admission to an MBA program, but to one degree or another, most business schools use them as part of the admissions process.

The GMAT uses a standardized set of criteria to evaluate the basic skills of college graduates, which allows graduate schools to compare and judge applicants. The test measures general verbal and math skills so that schools can assess an applicant's ability to succeed in a graduate-level environment.

• Quantitative section—this section measures mathematical skills and the ability to solve quantitative problems.
• Qualitative section—this section focuses on verbal skills, the ability to understand and interpret written materials, and basic English writing skills.
• Scoring—total scores range from 200 to 800, but scores lower than 300 and higher than 700 are unusual.
• Analytical Writing Assessment— this section requires test-takers to write two essays that measure the ability to think critically and communicate complex ideas through writing in English. This section is scored on a scale of 0 to 6, but scores lower than 2 and higher than 5 are unusual.
• Taking the test—until recently, the GMAT was available throughout the world as a paper-and-pencil test. Since October 1997, however, the GMAT has been available in North America and many other parts of the world only as a computer-adaptive test. (Research has shown that scores from the

paper-based test are comparable to those from the computer-based test.) The GMAT is offered by appointment many times each month at hundreds of locations worldwide. It is possible to schedule a test within a few days of taking it, but popular dates, such as weekends, fill up quickly. You should call the test center as early as possible to increase your chances of getting your preferred date. For more information, contact GMAT, Educational Testing Service, P.O. Box 6103, Princeton, NJ 08541-6103 (telephone: 609-771-7330; fax: 609-883-4349; Web site: http://www.gmat.org).

Professional Work Experience

Admission to selective, international business programs usually requires full-time, professional work experience prior to enrollment. While professional work experience is needed to provide a context for the interpretation and use of classroom material, students must also be able to contribute to class discussions and group projects in meaningful ways. Career success is the most effective way to prove your potential for leadership in a managerial capacity.

Personal Qualities

MBA programs want to enroll students who can lead people. The admissions committee seeks men and women who will eventually be responsible for the management of entire organizations. Leadership is one of the basic ingredients for success. Communication skills, initiative, and motivation can become the most important aspects of the admissions process. Personal qualities set the tone for the entire review of an application. It is the one part of an application that is most likely to distinguish a candidate in a compelling way.

The Interview

The interview is the one aspect of the admissions process that varies the most among schools. Some schools, like the Kellogg School at Northwestern, require all applicants to interview prior to admission. Others, such as Stanford's Graduate School of Business, do not interview any of their applicants. Most schools, like Wharton at the University of Pennsylvania, leave the decision to interview up to the applicant. It is one more part of the admissions process that the applicant can control. For those prospective students who do have the interview available to them, it is a highly recommended experience. It is also a great opportunity to take initiative in the admissions process.

If an interview is part of the admissions process, it can be an invaluable opportunity for the applicant to show the strengths and leadership qualities that most business schools are seeking in MBA candidates. The most effective and interesting interviews are those discussions that go beyond the information provided in the written application. Too often interviews remain focused solely on the candidate's resume. The meeting becomes nothing more than a redundancy in the evaluation of a candidacy. It is up to both the interviewer and the applicant to create an exchange of information that solicits useful information that will help the admissions committee understand the context of the choices that the applicant has made throughout life.

In Summary

Categories and labels do not play as significant a role in the process as most applicants assume. Prospective MBA students should take a high level of initiative during the admissions process, while exercising discretion when determining what information is most important for a school to properly evaluate their candidacy.

These guidelines are the first step in understanding the nature of the admissions process from the perspective of an admissions officer. It is vital to recognize that each school has its own policies and procedures in admissions. Careful research and communication will, fundamentally, have the greatest impact on the success of an MBA application.

GradAdvantage: Applying to Business School Just Got a Whole Lot Easier!

Thanks to a new, cutting-edge service developed by Educational Testing Service and Peterson's, and sponsored by the Graduate Management Admission Council, you can now apply to business schools on line. The new service, GradAdvantage, allows you to apply to as many schools as you wish, enter most of your personal data only once, and have your application arrive at the admission office with your secure Graduate Management Admission Test (GMAT) attached.

The GradAdvantage Alliance

GradAdvantage brings together the three major players in the business-school admission arena to develop an online service to make applying to schools easier for you.

Educational Testing Service (ETS), a private, nonprofit corporation headquartered in Princeton, NJ, develops, delivers, scores, and manages score reports for "high-stakes" tests. These tests include the SAT, GRE, GMAT, and TOEFL, to name only a few. For millions of American and international students, the results of these tests have helped determine which institution they attend. Celebrating its fiftieth anniversary this year, ETS is moving in new directions to simplify the admission process for students and institutions alike and to promote its mission of education access for all.

The Graduate Management Admission Council (GMAC), an association of the 130 most prestigious business schools worldwide, provides a variety of services to MBA students and business schools alike. GMAC sponsors diversity programs such as the Ph.D. Project and Destination MBA, outreach programs such as the MBA Forums, and professional development workshops for admission deans. Materials both in print and on CD, such as the MBAExplorer Web site, the computer-adaptive GMAT, and the MBA LOANS programs, show GMAC's commitment to promoting business school education and industry professionalism both in the U.S. and around the world.

Peterson's, America's largest education information/communications company, is a leading educational database publisher, the valued publishing partner of admission officers and academic deans at every level, a publisher of books and CDs, and a developer of online services designed to facilitate access to education and career guidance. Peterson's is known globally for the accuracy and breadth of its data, first in print, then in software, and now on line with Peterson's Web site, petersons.com. The company is a subsidiary of The Thomson Corporation, a $7.7-billion publishing and information company. At the foundation of most of its activities is the country's largest education data collection, covering kindergarten through executive training and adult education, which is revised and expanded annually.

The GradAdvantage Web Site: gradadvantage.org

At gradadvantage.org, you will find a wealth of information about business schools, financing options, and GMAT registration, as well as a variety of ways to prepare for taking the GMAT and applying to business schools. Click on "New and Registered User Login" to begin applying to business schools on line.

When you click on the "Program Search & Financing" tab at the bottom of the screen, you will find that you have two choices: links to mba.petersons.com and to MBAExplorer, the GMAC Web site. In MBAExplorer, you can delve into information about MBA programs around the world and find links to those institutions' Web sites, learn about financing your business school education, buy the Pre-MBA CD and

GMAT test-prep products at the GMAC online store, and check out GMAC's calendar of events.

Click on mba.petersons.com and search for the right business school for you by name, concentration, location, average GMAT score, and enrollment size or do keyword searches to look for particular MBA programs in Peterson's searchable database. Numerous In-Depth Descriptions include detailed program and faculty information. You can join Peterson's MBA discussion board, purchase books and CDs, and find information about distance-learning MBA programs, GMAT test preparation, and financing your education.

The Benefits to You

With GradAdvantage, you can complete your applications on line, save your work, and return to it later. You no longer have to find a typewriter or try to match application spacing with your computer printer. It's easy to revise answers or essays as you rethink the questions during the application process before you submit your application.

GradAdvantage will save you lots of time. You can enter most information into multiple applications at the same time. If, for example, you are applying to four schools, the information you supply in the "Biographical," "Education," "Activities," and "Employment" tabs automatically cross-fills into the corresponding data fields in the other three applications. You will only have to respond to questions on the "Programs" and the "Essay" tabs in each application.

You no longer have to rely on express mail or courier services to deliver your application to admission offices on time. On average, most MBA applicants have jobs and work on their applications late at night the week or two before applications are due. All you have to do is click on "Submit," and your application is on its way to the institutions you designate. GradAdvantage's modest $12-per-application fee costs less than many express services—and is much less hassle.

You can pay by credit card to further save you time. Just enter your American Express, MasterCard, or Visa credit card number on the "Finish" tab, and your application will arrive with its electronic payment attached.

Your secure GMAT scores will arrive already integrated into your application. ETS has worked closely with Peterson's to guarantee the security of score data. All you have to do is provide the information that is used to ensure that score matching is accurate.

You can work on your application anywhere as long as you can access the Web. All you have to do is remember the URL for the GradAdvantage service: gradadvantage. org. The platform- and browser-independent service works with both PCs and Macs and on both Internet Explorer and Netscape and requires no substantial upgrades in hardware or software.

You can also track the progress of each of your applications using GradAdvantage's "Application Manager" interface.

The Future of GradAdvantage

In the future, you will be able to find a host of new functionalities on GradAdvantage to further streamline the application process. To make your life even easier, on gradadvantage.org you will be able to:

• Request additional GMAT score reports

• Have your college transcripts and letters of recommendation electronically authenticated and sent to designated institutions

• Access international transcript-evaluation services

• Learn more about financing your MBA through a variety of financial aid services

• Discover more in-depth information about business schools you should consider in online MBA Forum events

Welcome to the new world of electronic applications! ETS, Peterson's, GMAC, and GradAdvantage's participating institutions encourage you to save time and money and apply on line using GradAdvantage.

Paying for Your MBA

by Bart Astor

Now that you've made a commitment to getting your MBA, the next question is likely to be "How will I pay for it?"

The first thing you will have to decide is whether you will go to school part-time and continue working full-time or go to school full-time while working part-time. About two thirds of MBA students get their degree while they continue working at a full-time job. And though it will take you longer to get your MBA this way, the costs are more manageable and the amount of money you'll need to borrow is kept to a minimum. Furthermore, if you work for one of the many companies that offers either full or partial tuition reimbursement to their employees, this will further reduce your expenses.

Some MBA programs, on the other hand, are only available to full-time students. If you go to one of these schools, it will be impossible for you to work full-time. Therefore, you will have to make some other arrangement to pay the expenses of your schooling and to find the necessary resources for your living expenses.

But it is not only possible to find the resources you will need, it is also quite likely. Unfortunately, though, for most full-time MBA students, most of the money is available through student loans. And the amount of debt an MBA student takes on can be quite sizable.

Most MBA students feel it is worthwhile to take on some debt to pay for a degree that they believe

---

TABLE 1: AVERAGE STARTING SALARY OFFERS FOR NON-MBA AND MBA GRADUATES

Degree (field of study)	Starting Salary Offer
BA (Arts & Letters)	$27,608
BA (Business)	31,437
MBA (nontechnical undergraduate degree)	$36,133
MBA (technical undergraduate degree)	47,760

Reprinted from the July 1998 Salary Survey, with permission from the National Association of Colleges and Employers (copyright holder).

---

will offer them considerable career advancement. In that sense, then, they view these costs as an investment in their earnings potential. And the numbers have consistently supported this claim. A quick look at Table 1: Average Starting Salary Offers for Non-MBA and MBA Graduates shows that the salary for holders of an MBA is 25 to 40 percent higher than for non-MBA graduates. Looking only at earnings potential, getting an MBA has certainly proved to be an excellent financial investment. And, of course, this does not even consider career opportunities or quality-of-life issues.

The Costs

Now let's look at the cost of getting your MBA degree. All students are required to pay some sort of tuition or fee to go to school (in some state-supported business schools, this may be called a "fee"). This can be a total amount for the year, regardless of the number of credits you take, or a per-credit amount. The annual tuition for a full-time student can range from $2000 or $4000 at some of the state-supported schools to well over $20,000 at some of the higher-priced business schools. In addition, some business schools require all students to pay fees for such things as student activities, health services, etc., much like you may have paid as an undergraduate.

Most business school students pay a little more for books and supplies than they did as an undergraduate. While the amount will differ at each school, the annual amount for a full-time student ranges from $500 to

$800. You will need a computer, so that will naturally add a considerable amount to the total cost. These are the two obvious additional expense categories you will face when you go to business school, and they are generally referred to as "direct costs." As a student, you will have to budget your expenses as carefully as you budget your time. You may need to cut back on the amount you spend on some discretionary items, such as clothing and entertainment.

Financial Aid

Most business school students take on considerable debt to pay their expenses since there are very few alternatives. Because you will most likely continue to work full-time while you pursue the MBA via distance learning programs, your salary in combination with your savings may be enough to avoid having to borrow very much. However, you may still decide it is better to borrow through a government-subsidized loan program than take the necessary funds out of your savings or current income.

Financial aid may be available for distance learning students in the form of federal or school-based student loans. Unfortunately, not all business schools offer financial aid to distance learning students. If you know that you will need financial assistance, you should contact the business school(s) of your choice to determine what type of financial aid programs they offer.

Another option for MBA students is to determine whether their employers are willing to finance part or all

Types of Financial Aid

Gift Aid (money you do not have to pay back)
Individual grants, scholarships, and fellowships (may be merit-based or need-based)
Sources: business schools, foundations, private companies, community groups

Tuition waivers (awarded by individual business schools)

Company employee educational benefits (a personnel benefit for employees of many large and some small companies. Generally covers only a portion of tuition)

Federal grants (very limited and based on need)

State grants (also very limited)

Loans
Federal Perkins Loan (need-based, lender is business school)

Federal Subsidized Stafford Loan (need-based, lender is a bank, savings & loan, etc.)

Federal Unsubsidized Stafford Loan (non-need-based)

Federal Direct Loan (similar to Stafford Loans; lender is the federal government)

Private loan programs (e.g., MBA Loans; Business Access Loans, etc.)

Tuition payment plans (private or school-based)

of the cost for the MBA degree program. Employer tuition reimbursement plans are one of the best forms of financial aid for MBA students. Prospective students should contact their employers to find out the availability and terms of company tuition reimbursement plans.

Applying for Financial Aid

If the school you are interested in attending offers financial aid to distance learning students, you will need to prepare for the application process. When you apply for financial aid, you are generally applying for both merit-based and need-based aid.

The application process has changed significantly in the past year or two, so even if you applied for financial aid as an undergraduate, you should pay close attention to the process described here.

To qualify for federal aid, most of which will be in the form of loans, every student is required to complete the Free Application for Federal Student Aid (FAFSA), either in paper or electronic form (either FAFSA Express, a diskette available from the government, or FAFSA on the Web). The paper form is available in both business school and undergraduate school financial aid offices (your local community college or even your local high school guidance office will have them available as well). The computer software, FAFSA Express, can be ordered by calling 800-801-0576. And you can access FAFSA on the Web at the Internet address: http://www.ed.gov.

Soon after January 1, 1999 (for students entering in the fall of 1999 or spring 2000), you should complete the FAFSA, which asks about your 1998 income and current assets. The application cannot be completed until after January 1, 1999.

Many business schools require that you complete a different application, the Financial Aid PROFILE, to begin the financial aid process and require the form to be completed much earlier, in October or November. The paper version of the PROFILE information is available from the same places as the FAFSA. It is also available on the Internet at http://www.collegeboard.org

You can also call a toll-free number (800-778-6888) and "register" your information, including which business schools you are applying to. You must also pay a registration fee of $5 plus $14.50 per school. A few weeks later you will receive your customized application form containing all of the questions asked by the schools you are applying to.

You may have to complete both the FAFSA and the PROFILE. The way to find out is check the PROFILE registration packet for the list of schools that require the PROFILE. You should also read the business school literature or ask someone in

the business school financial aid office to be certain.

A few business schools will have their own aid application or use yet a third form, called Need Access. This information will be noted in the brochures they send to you, so be sure to check the literature. Make certain you know if there are deadlines when applying for financial aid. Applying after a deadline can hurt your chances of qualifying for aid.

Once you have submitted an application, the business schools you have designated will receive an output showing an amount you can afford to contribute to your education, calculated based on your income and assets. This number is called the "Expected Family Contribution" (EFC). The EFC from the federal form is the official amount that determines whether you will qualify for federal aid. If this amount is less than the total cost of attendance of the MBA program, you have demonstrated need and will qualify for aid, again, usually low-cost, government-subsidized loans. The output from the PROFILE will give the school an estimate of your federal eligibility and will also give an expected contribution based on additional criteria you provided. This contribution will be used by those schools using the PROFILE to award their own funds. And, like the federal EFC, if your contribution is less than the total cost of the school, you qualify for need-based aid.

But even if your family contribution is higher than the cost of the school, you may still qualify for aid. There are government, institutional,

TABLE 2: ESTIMATED LOAN REPAYMENT SCHEDULE
Monthly Payments for Every $1000 Borrowed

Rate	5 years	10 years	15 years	20 years	25 years
5%	$18.87	$10.61	$ 7.91	$ 6.60	$ 5.85
8%	20.28	12.13	9.56	8.36	7.72
9%	20.76	12.67	10.14	9.00	8.39
10%	21.74	13.77	10.75	9.65	9.09
12%	22.24	14.35	12.00	11.01	10.53
14%	23.27	15.53	13.32	12.44	12.04

You can use this table to estimate your monthly payments on a loan for any of the five repayment periods (5, 10, 15, 20, and 25 years). The amounts listed are the monthly payments for a $1000 loan for each of the interest rates. To estimate your monthly payment, choose the closest interest rate and multiply the amount of the payment listed by the total amount of your loan and then divide by 1,000. For example, for a total loan of $15,000 at 9% to be paid back over 10 years, multiply $12.67 times 15,000 (190,050) divided by 1,000. This yields $190.05 per month.

and private loans available to students regardless of whether they have demonstrated need (such as the Federal Unsubsidized Stafford Loan, MBA Loans, and Business Access Loans). Although these loans ultimately cost borrowers more since they are not subsidized, they are still sources of income for you to pay your business school costs.

Your Credit History

Since most MBA students have to borrow to pay for their education, making sure you qualify for a loan is critical. For the most part that means your credit record must be free of default or delinquency. You can check your credit history with one or more of the following four major credit bureaus and clean up any adverse credit that appears. You can look up the local numbers in your phone book or call the numbers below:

Equifax
P.O. Box 105873
Atlanta, GA 30348
800-685-1111
Fax: 404-612-3150

CSC Credit Services
Consumer Assistance Center
P.O. Box 674402
Houston, TX 77267-4402
800-759-5979

Trans Union Corporation
P.O. Box 390
Springfield, PA 19064-0390
800-888-4213

Experian
P.O. Box 9530
Allen, TX 75013
888-397-3742

Debt Management

Although the limits on borrowing from federal and private programs are quite high, you will want to make sure you are not borrowing more than you will later be able to repay. Use Table 2 below to estimate your MBA school loan monthly payments. Then by estimating your income and the total amount you'll need to borrow for your MBA education, you can use Table 3 to determine whether your loan payments will be affordable.

TABLE 3: DEBT MANAGEMENT GUIDE

Total Outstanding Loan	Years in Repayment	Monthly Payment	Suggested Minimum Monthly Income
$10,000	10	$126	$ 840
20,000	10	253	1,687
30,000	10	380	2,533
40,000	10	506	3,373
50,000	10	633	4,220
20,000	20	179	1,193
30,000	20	270	1,800
40,000	20	360	2,400
50,000	20	450	3,000

Additional Information

For more information about financing your education, refer to the personnel office at the company for whom you work and the business school financial aid office. You can also obtain additional information on possible sources of aid from the following Peterson's publications.

• *Grants for Graduate and Postdoctoral Study*
• *Financing Graduate School*

For information about loan options, you can contact the following organizations:

The Access Group
P.O. Box 7400
Wilmington, DE 19803-0400
800-292-1330

Business and Professional Women's Foundation
Loan Programs
2012 Massachusetts Avenue, NW
Washington, DC 20036
202-293-1200

ConSern Loans for Education
205 Van Buren Street, Suite 200
Herndon, VA 22070
800-SOS-LOAN

The Education Resource Institute (TERI)
330 Stuart Street, Suite 500
Boston, MA 02116
800-255-TERI

MBA Loans
2400 Broadway, Suite 230
Santa Monica, CA 90404
800-366-6227

New England Education Loan Marketing Corporation
    (Nellie Mae)
50 Braintree Hill Park, Suite 300
Braintree, MA 02184
800-634-9308

USA Group Affinity Loan
P.O. Box 6182
Indianapolis, IN 46206
800-635-3785

Sallie Mae Smart Loan Consolidation
P.O. Box 1304
Merrifield, VA 22116-1304
800-524-9100

U.S. Department of Education
Office of Student Financial Assistance
400 Maryland Avenue
Washington, DC 20202
800-433-3243 (Federal Student Aid Information Center)

What You Need to Know About Distance Learning

By Sandra Davis, Marketing Manager, MBA Program, Athabasca University

Canada's Athabasca University has been an active participant and leader in the distance education revolution and was one of the first universities to launch an online MBA program. The University's business is distance education, and it began offering both distance degree and certificate programs in 1974. Since the launch of the electronic MBA in 1994, this program's student population has grown from 64 to 725. This rapid growth reflects a marketplace demand for not only graduate-level business education but also for alternatives to the traditional, full-time, on-campus MBA.

The ongoing developments in information technology—fiber-optic cables, satellites, personal computers, video and audio streaming products, and course development and testing software—are fundamentally changing the world of distance education. The old world of isolated learning while sitting among books and paper is falling away as a new world evolves where the boundaries of time and space can collapse, and students can link electronically to fellow students and professors around the world.

What is it that you need to know about distance education and learning and about yourself as a potential distance learner as you research various MBA programs? Universities that offer distance education programs and courses address these questions on a daily basis. Here are some of the more common questions.

What is distance learning?

Distance learning means that a student generally studies and works on courses away from a physical campus setting and a professor.

In the recent past, a student received study materials at home, studied alone, and submitted assignments to a professor through paper correspondence; at times, students and professors talked by telephone. A number of universities still deliver programs this way or offer this as an alternative study mode to students. With the advent of such technological innovations as satellite television, personal computers, and the

Internet, however, both study materials and interpersonal interaction have been significantly enhanced. Distance learning students can now:

• Receive both hard copy and electronic textbooks and readings, including CD-ROM–formatted materials
• Access video- and audio-enhanced learning materials via the Internet
• Attend televised lectures
• Attend videoconference classes that link students and professors from numerous geographic locations
• Use e-mail to communicate with fellow students and professors
• Participate in formalized chat room discussions in real time
• Participate in formalized, asynchronous electronic group discussions
• Complete team-based assignments electronically with fellow students who are located across the country and around the world
• Submit assignments and/or write exams electronically
• Conduct research and access university libraries and other important research sites via the Internet

The impact of these technological advancements means that distance education programs can be designed to ensure maximum student interaction and student-professor communication. Since the students that meet together in this environment can come from diverse geographic locations and have different backgrounds and experience, the interaction provides an enriched learning experience.

Why has distance learning grown in popularity recently?

The workplace is changing and demanding a higher skill level of its workers. Working adults require further formal learning to remain competitive in the rapidly changing marketplace and enhance their career opportunities. These same people do not want to interrupt their employment or earning power to return to a university setting on a full-time basis for studies.

Most adult learners who seek an MBA degree are looking for a program that is fully accredited and recognized and:

• Allows them to keep working and retain their earning power
• Relates to and influences their working environment
• Prepares them to deal strategically and effectively in their industry
• Offers academically sound and challenging courses
• Enhances their career opportunities
• Allows them to balance work, education, and family commitments effectively

How does distance learning typically work?

There is no typical delivery system. Rather, prospective students can choose from a number of delivery models. Some of the more common approaches are described below.

1. *Individual learning* In this model, students complete the MBA course work totally on their own, with no contact with other students and limited contact with

professors. For example, Herriot-Watt University, Edinburgh, Scotland, distributes MBA courses via mail. Students purchase courses one at a time, set their own pace, study alone, and communicate with professors by mail, e-mail, and/or fax. ISIM University in Denver, Colorado, offers MBA students with limited Internet access guided, self-study courses as an optional mode of program delivery.

2. *Alternate weekend classroom sessions* While students are responsible for completing the bulk of their course work off campus, they meet as a group on alternate weekends with the professor for classroom-based sessions. This method allows face-to-face interaction and enables students to participate in lectures and discussions, complete team assignments, and write exams in a classroom setting. It also provides an opportunity for students to network with other managers and professionals who live and work in the geographic region. Students who choose this type of program must be able to commit to the classroom schedule. Often, these classes begin on a Friday and require students to make special arrangements with their employers for time off. For example, Duke University's Fuqua School of Business in Durham, North Carolina, offers a program called the WEMBA (Weekend Executive MBA).

3. *Alternate weekend videoconference classroom sessions* This system is almost identical to model 2, above, except that the face-to-face interaction is broadened, and students study and network with others from across the state or nation. The professors usually present materials and coordinate classroom discussion from a studio that is located at the university's home campus, and the class is transmitted by satellite. Students view a number of monitors that present the professor and students from the various classroom sites. Team projects are possible and usually organized by site, and exams can be delivered in the classroom setting. For example, Queens School of Business at Queens University in Kingston, Ontario, Canada, offers a National Videoconference Executive MBA program.

4. *Online* Students complete course work and can engage in synchronous (real-time) or asynchronous group discussions on line. Professors can also structure the courses so that students can complete team projects and/or write exams in the electronic environment. With the availability of multimedia CD-ROMs and computerized video and audio clips, course materials are being developed in these media as well.

While there may be no face-to-face encounters in each course, this does not mean that student-student or student-professor interaction is compromised. Educational software products, such as Lotus Learning Space® or Internet-developed course chat rooms, ensure maximum interaction among students and professors. Students in online programs have the opportunity to network with fellow managers and professionals from across a number of states or around the world.

In synchronously delivered programs, students must be able to participate in courses at set times and be conscious of time zone changes. In asynchronous programs, students participate at the time of day that is convenient for them, and time zones are not a factor. In online programs, students can take the program with them wherever they happen to be. For example, the Centre for Innovative Management at Athabasca University in St. Albert, Canada, offers an asynchronously delivered MBA program that links students and professors from around the world.

Regardless of the method of delivery, most MBA programs:

• Have some form of residency requirement built in. This residency requirement can vary greatly from institution to institution, and prospective students need to be sure that they can meet any and all residency requirements.
• Require students to have access to computers and the Internet. A university will specify the required hardware and software. In some instances, the software and/or hardware is provided as part of the tuition package. For example, Athabasca University provides students with the required software,

while Queen's University provides students with both the hardware and the software. The program price often reflects the cost of including these products.

What are the advantages of distance learning over a traditional MBA program?

Focus on application of concepts. Most distance MBA students are highly experienced managers and professionals who bring a wealth of experience to their learning. As a result, there is a better focus on the application of the course concepts.

Direct relevance to and application in the workplace. Many students are able to enhance their careers and provide immediate benefit to their employers while they are in the program.

Networking and peer support in most programs. Students are able to discuss current work issues not only with the professors but also with their fellow students, thereby obtaining a broad spectrum of feedback. In online programs, students can develop professional networks that can stretch across a nation and around the globe.

Group-work skills honed in most programs. The online programs, such as the one at Athabasca University, also provide opportunities for students to hone these skills in an electronic environment, as their teams are comprised of people from across the country or around the world.

Maintain employment and standard of living. Students do not have to leave their jobs or forfeit their current standard of living to obtain a graduate business degree.

What characteristics are common to successful distance learning students?

Successful MBA distance learning students usually share a number of characteristics. They:

- Are self-motivated and self-directed learners
- Can work in groups
- Are usually highly experienced and bring a variety of real-world examples to the learning
- Have the ability to integrate theory with application
- Have computer skills (Successful students start the program with a good grounding in computer basics and a working knowledge of some word processing and spreadsheet software.)
- Have good time-management skills and are able to balance work, study, and family commitments
- Are psychologically well prepared for the time commitment and the work
- Have strong family support for their goal of obtaining an MBA while working

What should you look for when selecting a program?

University Accreditation First, determine that the university is fully recognized and accredited within its jurisdiction.

Program Quality Since the vast majority of distance MBA students are experienced in the work world, prospective students want to ensure that the program's courses:

- Are developed with industry input
- Are current and relevant
- Offer a balance between theory and application
- Provide opportunities for assignments to be linked to the workplace
- Focus on high-level knowledge and skills (e.g., strategic thinking, decision making, ethics, managerial accounting)
- Provide teamwork and/or group discussion opportunities
- Provide networking opportunities

Academic Profile What percentage of professors:

- Have doctorates
- Have industry experience
- Have international experience
- Are women

Student Profile Ask for the program's student profile, which includes such things as average age, men-women ratio, average years of work and/or managerial experience, industry sector breakdown, and province, state, national, and international participation rates. The more experienced the students and the more diverse their backgrounds, the richer the learning experience.

Student Support This is critical. Students who study at a distance require a high level of academic, administrative, and technical support. Are performance measurements established to ensure that you get the support you need? For example, with Athabasca University's MBA program, academics must respond to every student's questions within 24 hours.

Does there appear to be a commitment to student service? Are you treated with respect and courtesy? Are staff members helpful and informative? Do you get the advice you need when you need it? Will you be asked for feedback about the quality of administrative, technical, and academic support you receive once you start the program?

Equipment Requirements Is equipment provided, or must you purchase it before starting? If the university changes the equipment requirements during the course of the program, how does this affect you both operationally and financially?

Costs What does the program cost and what does that cost include—application fee, admission fee, tuition, residency session fees, travel costs, textbooks, software, hardware? What additional costs must be borne by the student (i.e., textbooks or travel costs to and from residency sessions).

Time Required to Complete the Program How long are students given to complete the program? What is the average length of time it takes for students to complete the program?

Drop-Out Rates What is the program's drop-out rate?

Residency Requirements Does the program require you to attend orientation sessions, summer or weekend schools, or international study trips? What is the number of required sessions, schools, or trips and their duration?

Portability and Flexibility of the Program If your work commitments require frequent travel, can the MBA program accommodate your learning while you are away? If you are transferred to another city, state, or country, can you continue the program? If not, will the courses you have taken to-date transfer to another institution? If work or family events require you to temporarily stop studies, can the program accommodate this interruption? If so, how?

What do students say about their MBA distance learning experiences?

These samples from Athabasca University illustrate how distance education is meeting the needs of people who desire an alternative to traditional programs.

"I live in Cyprus and work in Russia. This program offered me the opportunity to enter into a recognized business program and maintain my employment and lifestyle. The program itself far exceeded my expectations. The experience is directly applicable to my current responsibilities as General Director in an oil and gas venture project. The theoretical and shared practical knowledge of the other students has made this a worthwhile initiative."

—Les Kondratoff, Halliburton International Inc., Moscow, Russia

"Working toward an MBA has helped me as a middle manager to appreciate the bigger corporate strategic picture and to understand the implications of that strategy for the different functional areas across the company. Because assignments almost always relate to the business

world you are in, they bring a dimension to the learning that is often missing—the application to the real world."
—Susan McKay, West Kootenay Power Ltd., Trail, British Columbia, Canada

"*The online MBA program at Athabasca has exceeded my expectations. Compared to conventional classroom instruction, the program's innovative structure provides greater interaction with students, faculty, and staff. The flexibility of the program allows me to pursue a high-quality, graduate education and meet commitments to work and family.*"
—Tim Nerenz, Lake Shore Inc., Kingsford, Michigan

"*At the start of the program, my only concern was a lack of student interaction and networking opportunities, and my experience has been quite the opposite. The opportunity to work in teams on line has been a very valuable experience, and the need for online interaction will become increasingly important in our global business environment. Combined with summer and weekend schools and optional weeklong residential electives, this program offers the best of all worlds!*"
—Mitch W. Fix, TELUS Residential Services, Edmonton, Alberta, Canada

Returning to School for Your MBA

by Barbara B. Reinhold, Ed.D., Director, Career Development, Smith College

Some decisions can be made and implemented quickly—you can often choose a new car, a new place to live, or even a new relationship rather impetuously and have it work out just fine. For the returning student, however, the process of deciding, applying to school, and then earning an MBA is seldom simple. It has to be done with a great deal of forethought and awareness of the considerable sacrifice required.

The good news about being a more mature student is that you'll probably get much more out of it, because there is more of you to take to the classroom—more experience, better judgment, clearer goals, and more appreciation for learning. The bad news is that your life will be more "squeezed" than it would have been before you took on all of life's responsibilities, particularly balancing work and family. In general, however, later is often better than sooner when it comes to getting an MBA.

For mature women and men alike, there are many things to consider before upending your life to pursue an MBA. First, be sure you really need one. It is silly to waste your time and resources being "retooled" in an MBA program if your career goals could be accomplished just as easily by taking targeted courses, getting more training and supervision through your employer, or using your connections to enter a different field or organization and move up. If you are trying to determine if an MBA is really the key to where you want to go, find ways to network with people whose lives and career goals are similar to yours. You might discover that a variety of routes could lead you to your desired goal.

It's essential that you make your own decision about whether and where to apply, using a blend of logic and intuition. Though an MBA requires strong quantitative skills, you'll also need good organizational, decision-making, and communication skills. For returning students, success in an MBA program is often due more to life and work experience than technical knowledge alone. You have more information, more common sense, and more self-awareness at your disposal than you did as an undergraduate student. Use these assets along with your intuition in deciding whether this is really right for you now.

It's important also to be an informed and demanding customer on the front end of the process. Be sure to ask hard questions about how well a school is prepared to respond to the particular concerns you might have. The ball will be in their court later; in the first half of the game, however, be aggressive about getting the information you need. For more mature students, the philosophy, resources, and services of the school can be much more important than ranking or reputation.

The application stage is also a great time to practice your marketing skills. This may be the first of many times when you'll have to convince someone of your worth. For returning students this is often frightening. Some have been out of the job market for awhile, while others either want to change careers or are feeling stuck at a career plateau. Any of these situations is likely to leave you feeling less than competitive. This is a good time to figure out what you really have to offer to a particular school and to adjust to the notion of lifelong self-advocacy.

As you begin the difficult task of self-assessment, be honest about your strengths and weaknesses. If your technical, quantitative, or communication competencies are not what they should be in order for you to begin course work in a confident frame of mind, spend a year or so coming up to speed in these areas. Although

you'll be taking accounting, statistics, and computer courses as part of the core requirements, it's best to be comfortable with these basic disciplines before you enroll.

Once enrolled, you can do two things to make your life easier. First, take an honest look at your own learning style. Try to determine which methods work best for you; use methods that fit your personality—outlines, memorizing, listening to tapes, discussing concepts with other people, etc. Be proactive and establish a routine. As a returning student with many other life responsibilities, you'll need to take a different approach to studying than you did in undergraduate school.

You'll also find that connecting with classmates is a critical part of doing well. You may be assigned to project teams, but it's a good idea to seek out your own support group as well. Form at-a-distance study groups, even though it may seem you can't spare the time. In business school, as in business itself, collaboration and networking are everything!

Becoming a student again is a great adventure—earning an MBA will tax you, test you, stretch you, and reward you, but only you can know if it's right for you. When you applied to college as a high school student, you thought you had all the answers. What's different now is that, although you still don't have all the answers, you probably know much more than you think.

TEN TIPS FOR RETURNING STUDENTS

DECIDING

1. Be sure an MBA is the best route to where you're going—don't embark on a trip until your destination is clear.

2. Make your own decision, using a blend of logic and intuition.

3. Be a discerning customer; ask hard questions about which programs best meet your specific needs.

ARRIVING

4. Learn to market yourself; don't launch the campaign until you're ready.

5. Be sure your support system is in order—at home and at work.

6. Review your skills—technical, quantitative, written, and oral. If you're not really ready to do well yet, take an extra year to polish those skills.

7. Measure your confidence level—if it's weak, consider counseling to learn how to manage your anxieties and self-doubts.

8. Get your life in good shape before you begin—paying attention to nutrition, exercise, relationships, and all the other things you'll need to sustain you.

THRIVING

9. Ascertain your most effective learning style (from your own self-assessment or more formalized measurements, such as the Learning Styles Inventory or the Myers-Briggs Type Inventory) and design routines and study regimens that best fit your style.

10. Find a group of friends/colleagues right away; collaboration is the key to succeeding and staying healthy through one of the most demanding experiences you'll ever have—even at a distance.

ALFRED UNIVERSITY
College of Business
Alfred, New York

Alfred University, founded in 1836, is an independent-nonprofit university. It is accredited by the Middle States Association of Colleges and Schools. The College of Business first offered graduate business distance learning courses in 1998. In 1997–98, it offered 3 graduate business courses at a distance.

Course delivery sites Courses are delivered to College Center of the Finger Lakes (Corning).

Media Courses are delivered via videoconferencing, e-mail. Students and teachers may interact via videoconferencing, e-mail.

Geographic service area/restrictions Programs are available locally.

Services Distance learners have access to library services, the campus computer network, e-mail services, academic advising, career placement assistance at a distance.

Typical costs Tuition of $405 per credit hour.

Registration Students may register by mail, fax, phone, e-mail.

Contact Dr. Daniel Acton, Director, MBA, Alfred University, College of Business, Saxon Drive, Alfred, NY 14802. *Telephone:* 607-871-2646. *Fax:* 607-871-2114. *E-mail:* facton@bigvax. alfred.edu.

DEGREE & CERTIFICATE PROGRAMS

Master of Business Administration (MBA)

Application requirements *Prior education:* Baccalaureate degree.

AMBER UNIVERSITY
Garland, Texas

Amber University, founded in 1971, is an independent-religious nondenominational upper-level institution. It is accredited by the Southern Association of Colleges and Schools. It first offered graduate business distance learning courses in 1995. In 1997–98, it offered 25 graduate business courses at a distance. In the fall of 1997, there were 50 students enrolled in distance learning graduate-level business courses and programs.

Course delivery sites Students can receive instruction anywhere.

Media Courses are delivered via computer software, World Wide Web, print. Students and teachers may meet in person or interact via mail, telephone, fax, e-mail, World Wide Web. The following equipment may be required: a computer with a modem.

Geographic service area/restrictions Students are predominately from within Texas.

Services Distance learners have access to library services, e-mail services, academic advising at a distance.

Typical costs Tuition of $450 per course.

Registration Students may register by mail, fax, phone, e-mail, World Wide Web.

Contact Dr. Algia Allen, Vice President for Academic Services, Amber University, 1700 Eastgate, Garland, TX 75041. *Telephone:* 972-279-6511, Ext. 135. *Fax:* 972-279-9773. *E-mail:* webteam@amberu.edu. *Web site:* http://amberu.edu.

DEGREE & CERTIFICATE PROGRAMS

Master of Arts (MA)

In the fall of 1997 there were 30 students enrolled in this program.

Geographic service area/restrictions Program is available statewide.

Application requirements *Prior education:* Baccalaureate degree. *Other requirements:* college transcripts.

Completion requirements 36 credits are required.

INDIVIDUAL COURSE SUBJECT AREAS

Graduate
Management; Management Information Systems

AMERICAN COLLEGE
The Richard D. Irwin Graduate School
Bryn Mawr, Pennsylvania

American College is an independent-nonprofit graduate institution. It is accredited by the Middle States Association of Colleges and Schools. The Richard D. Irwin Graduate School first offered graduate business distance learning courses in 1974. In 1997–98, it offered 18 graduate business courses at a distance.

Course delivery sites Students can receive instruction anywhere.

Media Courses are delivered via print. Students and teachers may meet in person or interact via mail, telephone, fax, e-mail.

Geographic service area/restrictions Programs are available nationwide.

Services Distance learners have access to library services, academic advising, tutoring at a distance.

Credit-earning options Students may transfer credits from another institution or may earn credits through examinations.

Typical costs Tuition of $490 per course. Some students may need to pay some additional fees depending on the area of study.

Registration Students may register by mail, fax, phone, World Wide Web.

Contact Office of Student Services, American College, 270 South Bryn Mawr Avenue, Bryn Mawr, PA 19010.

Telephone: 610-526-1490. *Fax:* 610-526-1465. *E-mail:* studentservices@amercoll.edu. *Web site:* http://www.amercoll.edu.

DEGREE & CERTIFICATE PROGRAMS

Master of Science in Financial Services (MSFS)

Application requirements *Prior education:* Baccalaureate degree. *Other requirements:* college transcripts, an application fee of $275, admission/registration form.

Completion requirements 36 credits are required. *Maximum time for completion:* seven years.

On-campus requirements Students must complete 12 credits during two on-campus residencies.

Graduate Certificate

Application requirements *Prior education:* Baccalaureate degree. *Other requirements:* registration form.

Completion requirements 9 credits are required.

American College

INDIVIDUAL COURSE SUBJECT AREAS

Graduate
Financial Management/Planning;
Taxation

Noncredit
Financial Management/Planning;
Taxation

ATHABASCA UNIVERSITY
Centre for Innovative Management
Athabasca, Alberta, Canada

Athabasca University, founded in 1970, is a province-supported comprehensive institution. It is provincially chartered. The Centre for Innovative Management first offered graduate business distance learning courses in 1994. In 1997–98, it offered 20 graduate business courses at a distance. In the fall of 1997, there were 472 students enrolled in distance learning graduate-level business courses and programs.

Course delivery sites Students can receive instruction anywhere.

Media Courses are delivered via computer software, World Wide Web, e-mail, print. Students and teachers may meet in person or interact via telephone, e-mail, World Wide Web, Lotus Notes. The following equipment may be required: a computer (486 or better) with CD-ROM and a sound card with speakers, a minimum 16MB of RAM and a minimum of 500 MB minimum of free space on the hard drive, a 28.8K modem, Windows 95, and a high quality printer.

Geographic service area/restrictions Programs are available worldwide. Students must meet the admissions standards for the MBA program.

Services Distance learners have access to library services, e-mail services, academic advising at a distance.

Credit-earning options Students may transfer credits from another institution or may earn credits through portfolio assessment.

Typical costs Tuition of $395.83 per credit plus mandatory fees of $11.45 per credit. Tuition is in Canadian dollars.

Registration Students may register by mail, fax, e-mail, World Wide Web.

Contact Ms. Shelly Lynes, Manager of Registration, Records and Graduate Student Affairs, Athabasca University, 301-22 Sir Winston Churchill Avenue, St. Albert, AB T8N 1B4, Canada. *Telephone:* 403-459-1144. *Fax:* 403-459-2093. *E-mail:* cimoffice@athabascau.ca. *Web site:* http://www.athabascau.ca.

DEGREE & CERTIFICATE PROGRAMS

Master of Business Administration (MBA)

In the fall of 1997 there were 472 students enrolled in this program. In 1996–97, 45 degrees were earned at a distance through this program.

Application requirements *Prior education:* a baccalaureate degree and/or professional designation. *Other requirements:* college transcripts, an essay or personal statement, letter(s) of recommendation, an application fee of $100 Canadian dollars, detailed resume, managerial work experience of at least three years, or professional designation and at least five years of managerial experience, or 8–10 years managerial experience.

Completion requirements 48 credits are required. *Maximum time for completion:* six years.

On-campus requirements Students must attend a seven day summer school conducted at various locations throughout Canada and two weekend schools on campus.

ATHABASCA UNIVERSITY

Athabasca University
Canada's Open University

Centre for Innovative Management

Online M.B.A. and Advanced Graduate Diploma in Management Programs
St. Albert, Alberta, Canada

THE UNIVERSITY

Since 1974, Athabasca University has specialized and become a world leader in the delivery of distance education courses. The University's strategic vision is to increase opportunities for accessible, high-quality, individualized distance-delivered education, accreditation, and training. The University offers a comprehensive list of more than 400 credit courses in a wide variety of disciplines, undergraduate degree programs, postdiplomas, University certificate programs, and graduate studies programs.

DISTANCE LEARNING PROGRAM

Students of the M.B.A. program come from the private sector of small, medium, and large organizations; public-sector institutions; and not-for-profit organizations. It is a flexible program that allows students to study from home, work, or the road while they continue with their careers.

The aim of the M.B.A. program is to provide students with a wide range of functional management skills. These skills not only improve a student's management delivery, but also provide insight into effective team management strategies and sound de-

cision making. Today's manager is a strategic leader who understands how to create and maintain a productive working environment.

The M.B.A. program requires students to complete ten courses, two electives, two comprehensive examinations, and one applied project and to attend a weeklong summer school and two weekend schools. The program is structured as a sequence of three phases, each building on the work completed in the previous phase(s).

Students normally complete the M.B.A. program in 2½ to 3 years. The regulations state that students must complete their M.B.A. studies within six years of their initial enrollment in the program.

DELIVERY MEDIA

The M.B.A. uses Lotus Notes®, a groupware product that enables students to access course information and materials, conduct group discussions, complete teamwork projects, and submit course work electronically. Students and faculty and staff members are all connected, creating an interactive learning environment while giving students the support and services they need.

The Centre delivers its summer and weekend schools at varying locations. To date, such schools have been held in a number of different cities across Canada.

SPECIAL PROGRAMS

The Advanced Graduate Diploma in Management (AGDM) is designed to meet the ongoing educational needs of managers who do not wish to pursue an M.B.A. The program is identical to phase one of the M.B.A. program and is taken with the M.B.A. students. Students who successfully complete the AGDM are eligible for admission to phases two and three of the M.B.A. program.

The M.B.A. in agriculture is a program that is jointly delivered by Canada's Athabasca University and the University of Guelph.

FACULTY

Six full-time and 45 part-time academics act as coaches, mentors, and guides to students in the program. Full-time faculty members work from the Centre offices located in St. Albert, while the part-time academics work from different locations in Canada, the United States, and Britain. Eighty percent of academics hold doctoral degrees, and most have industry and/or international experience in their areas of specialization.

CREDIT OPTIONS

Requests for advanced standing for courses completed at other institutions must be made at the time of admission to the program. The committee that reviews admissions requires official transcripts and, in some cases, detailed course descriptions in order to evaluate and approve such requests.

Subject to appropriate approval, students may take one of their elective courses from another postsecondary institution, providing the course is relevant and equivalent to courses in the M.B.A. program.

ADMISSION

An applicant must either have obtained a first degree at an accredited university or college and have completed at least three years of acceptable managerial or professional experience or hold an acceptable professional designation and have completed at least five years of acceptable managerial or professional experience that shows progressive responsibility. Applicants who hold neither a degree nor a professional designation can seek admission into the program via the Advanced Graduate Diploma in Management route and must have eight to ten years of substantive experience in operating a business or managing in an organization. Successful completion of the AGDM is accepted as an academic credential for admission to the M.B.A. program.

TUITION AND FEES

For the 1998–99 academic year, the program cost is Can$19,550 for the M.B.A. and Can$9050 for the AGDM. This includes the registration fee, the admission fee, tuition fees, and all required software and textbooks. For programs delivered outside of Canada, all fees must be paid in U.S. dollars.

APPLYING

Application deadlines are June 30 for a September program start, October 30 for January, and February 26 for May. Applicants must submit a general application form; an application letter detailing why they wish to study in the program, what background equips them to study in the M.B.A. or AGDM program, and what they hope the program offers in terms of personal development, career development, and learning; names, addresses, and contact numbers of three references (special-circumstance applications require three letters of reference); a current resume; transcripts; confirmed access to computer equipment; and the Can$100 application fee.

CONTACT

Centre for Innovative Management
Athabasca University
301-22 Sir Winston Churchill
   Avenue
St. Albert, Alberta T8N 1B4
Canada
Telephone: 403-459-1144
            800-561-4650 (toll-free)
Fax: 403-459-2093
      800-561-4660 (toll-free)
E-mail: cimoffice@athabascau.ca

AUBURN UNIVERSITY
College of Business
Auburn University, Alabama

Auburn University, founded in 1856, is a state-supported university. It is accredited by the Southern Association of Colleges and Schools. The College of Business first offered graduate business distance learning courses in 1984. In 1997–98, it offered 58 graduate business courses at a distance. In the fall of 1997, there were 145 students enrolled in distance learning graduate-level business courses and programs.

Course delivery sites Students can receive instruction anywhere.

Media Courses are delivered via videotapes, World Wide Web, e-mail, print. Students and teachers may interact via telephone, e-mail, World Wide Web. The following equipment may be required: a TV and VCR and/or a computer with access to the Internet and email.

Geographic service area/restrictions Programs are available nationwide.

Services Distance learners have access to library services, the campus computer network, e-mail services, academic advising, tutoring, career placement assistance, bookstore at a distance.

Credit-earning options Students may transfer credits from another institution or may earn credits through examinations.

Typical costs Tuition of $225 per hour. Costs may vary by number of

credits taken. Financial aid is available to distance learners.

Registration Students may register by phone, World Wide Web.

Contact Joye Hughes, Program Advisor, Auburn University, 202 Ramsay Hall, Auburn University, AL 36849-5336. *Telephone:* 888-844-5300. *Fax:* 334-844-2519. *E-mail:* jhughes@eng. auburn.edu. *Web site:* http://www. mba.business.auburn.edu.

DEGREE & CERTIFICATE PROGRAMS

Master of Business Administration (MBA)

In the fall of 1997 there were 145 students enrolled in this program. In 1996–97, 35 degrees were earned at a distance through this program.

Application requirements *Prior education:* Baccalaureate degree. *Other requirements:* GMAT, college transcripts, an essay or personal statement, letter(s) of recommendation, an application fee of $25, computer literacy.

Completion requirements 60–88 quarter hours. *Maximum time for completion:* five years.

On-campus requirements The MBA team case analysis requires a minimum of three days on campus.

AUBURN UNIVERSITY

College of Business

Video-Based Outreach MBA
Auburn University, Alabama

THE UNIVERSITY

Auburn University, as a part of its land-grant tradition, is committed to meeting the needs of industry and individuals across the nation through instruction, research, and extension. The College of Business is particularly sensitive to the needs of professionals who wish to maintain and upgrade their skills even though they balance family and job responsibilities that prohibit them from returning to campus. Chartered in 1856, the University is located in the friendly, small-town environment of Auburn, Alabama. The University is home to 21,550 students (including 2,900 graduate students), 1,100 faculty members, and more than fifty major academic buildings. Auburn University courses are accredited by the Southern Association of Colleges and Schools. The M.B.A. program is fully accredited by AACSB–The International Association for Management Education.

DISTANCE LEARNING PROGRAM

Since 1990, the Auburn M.B.A. program has been available through the Video-Based Outreach MBA program. More than 150 students (250 students are currently enrolled) have completed their degree through this flexible, innovative program. This program offers professionals the op-portunity to continue their education while maintaining full-time employment, whatever their location. Video-Based Outreach MBA students receive the same instruction as on-campus students and complete all class assignments and tests. Students from across the United States who represent Fortune 500 companies, small firms, and all branches of the military are currently earning an Auburn M.B.A. through the Video-Based Outreach MBA program.

DELIVERY MEDIA

The Auburn University campus is equipped with several video classroom studios. M.B.A. courses are held in these rooms so they can be outreach classes as well. Classes in these rooms are recorded on multiple VCRs while the class is being conducted. The resulting videotapes are sent out within 24 hours, and students usually receive them within two to four days. Students view the tapes and are expected to return them within two weeks. The homework assignments and tests are the same as those assigned to on-campus students and must be completed and mailed in by the specific due dates. A test proctor, usually someone located at the student's place of business, monitors all exams. All questions regarding the courses can be addressed to the faculty through e-mail, mail, or, during designated times, the telephone. E-mail and Internet access are required for someone to successfully complete the program.

SPECIAL PROGRAMS
Video-Based Outreach MBA students have access to the same campus services and special programs as on-campus students. The Auburn M.B.A. program currently supports international exchange programs in the Czech Republic, Japan, Germany, and France. An internship program is also available.

FACULTY
The M.B.A. faculty members excel as instructors and researchers, with 89 full-time and 8 part-time members. All faculty members have doctoral degrees and are actively involved in research and consulting, keeping at the forefront of their disciplines.

STUDENT SERVICES
Services available to Video-Based Outreach MBA students include academic advising, career counseling/planning, job fairs, career placement, access to an electronic job bank, resume preparation, and referral.

CREDIT OPTIONS
The M.B.A. program ranges from 60 to 88 credit hours, depending upon the student's undergraduate degree, grades, and any relevant graduate work. The student has five years to complete the program; however, the average length of time in the Video-Based Outreach MBA program is three years. Auburn can only accept

transfer hours from other programs that are accredited by AACSB–The International Association of Management Education. Courses must have been taken within the last five years and completed with a grade no lower than a B. Concentrations are available in health-care administration, finance, human resources, management information systems, marketing, operations management, and technology management.

ADMISSION
Applicants to the M.B.A. program must hold a bachelor's degree from an accredited college or university. Admission criteria include undergraduate transcripts, GMAT scores, TOEFL scores (international students), an M.B.A. application, a Graduate School application, and three letters of recommendation. The average GPA for M.B.A. students is 3.2, and the average GMAT score is 595.

TUITION AND FEES
All Video-Based Outreach MBA students pay the same fees regardless of residency status. The course fee is $225 per quarter hour. There is also a graduation fee of $20.

FINANCIAL AID
Financial Aid is available to both full- and part-time students. Most Video-Based Outreach MBA students are supported through employer tuition reimbursement plans; however, an increasing number of students apply for federal financial aid.

APPLYING

Applications are accepted for fall, winter, spring, and summer quarters, and students are encouraged to submit completed applications well in advance of the deadlines (August 1, November 15, February 15, and May 1, respectively). The MBA Admissions Committee reviews completed applications, and students are generally informed of their status within two weeks of the receipt of all elements of the application. There is an application fee of $25 for U.S. residents and $50 for international students.

CONTACT

Ms. Joye Hughes, Program Advisor
Video-Based Outreach MBA
202 Ramsey Hall
Auburn University, Alabama 36849
Telephone: 888-844-5300 (toll-free)
Fax: 334-844-2519
E-mail: jhughes@eng.auburn.edu
Web site: http://www.mba.business.
  auburn.edu

AURORA UNIVERSITY

School of Business and Professional Studies

Aurora, Illinois

Aurora University, founded in 1893, is an independent-nonprofit comprehensive institution. It is accredited by the North Central Association of Colleges and Schools. The School of Business and Professional Studies first offered graduate business distance learning courses in 1998. In 1997–98, it offered 2 graduate business courses at a distance.

Course delivery sites Students can receive instruction anywhere.

Media Courses are delivered via computer software, World Wide Web, e-mail, print. Students and teachers may meet in person or interact via mail, telephone, fax, e-mail, World Wide Web. The following equipment may be required: a computer (486 or better) with Windows, a printer, a CD-ROM drive, a modem and a soundcard. The computer must also meet specific requirements.

Geographic service area/restrictions Programs are available worldwide. Internet access is required and courses are offered in English only.

Services Distance learners have access to e-mail services, academic advising, computer system technical information at a distance.

Typical costs Tuition of $1176 per course.

Registration Students may register by mail.

Contact Dr. Laurence J. Quick, Director, W. Edwards Deming Center for Ethical Leadership, Aurora University, 347 South Gladstone Avenue, Aurora, IL 60506-4892. *Telephone:* 630-844-4888. *Fax:* 630-844-7830. *E-mail:* lquick@admin.aurora.edu. *Web site:* http://www.aurora.edu.

DEGREE & CERTIFICATE PROGRAMS

Advanced Certificate in Deming Management

Geographic service area/restrictions Students must have an excellent command of the English language and a computer with access to the Internet.

Application requirements *Prior education:* Baccalaureate degree. *Other requirements:* college transcripts, an essay or personal statement, an application fee of $100, work experience.

Completion requirements 21 semester hours are required.

Certificate in Deming Management

Geographic service area/ restrictions Students must have an excellent command of the English language and a computer with access to the Internet.

Application requirements *Prior education:* Baccalaureate degree. *Other requirements:* college transcripts, an essay or personal statement, an application fee of $100, work experience.

Completion requirements 12 semester hours are required.

INDIVIDUAL COURSE SUBJECT AREAS

Graduate

Financial Management/Planning; Human Resources; Leadership; Marketing; Production Management; Quality Management

BALL STATE UNIVERSITY
College of Business
Muncie, Indiana

Ball State University, founded in 1918, is a state-supported university. It is accredited by the North Central Association of Colleges and Schools. The College of Business first offered graduate business distance learning courses in 1983. In 1997–98, it offered 29 graduate business courses at a distance. In the fall of 1997, there were 171 students enrolled in distance learning graduate-level business courses and programs.

Course delivery sites Courses are delivered to your workplace, military bases, high schools, hospitals, Huntington College (Huntington), Indiana University East (Richmond), Indiana University–Purdue University Indianapolis (Indianapolis), Taylor University (Upland), Tri-State University (Angola), University of Evansville (Evansville), University of Southern Indiana (Evansville), Vincennes University (Vincennes), several Ivy Tech State College campuses throughout Indiana plus 48 sites in Indiana, New Jersey and Kentucky.

Media Courses are delivered via interactive television. Students and teachers may meet in person or interact via mail, telephone, fax, e-mail, interactive television, World Wide Web. The following equipment may be required: a computer with access to the Internet.

Geographic service area/restrictions Programs are available at sites in Kentucky, New Jersey and Indiana. Students must be at a location in which satellite equipment is installed to view classes or at a location that wishes to install the equipment.

Services Distance learners have access to library services, the campus computer network, e-mail services, academic advising, career placement assistance, bookstore at a distance.

Credit-earning options Students may transfer credits from another institution.

Typical costs Tuition of $126 per credit.

Registration Students may register by mail, fax, phone, e-mail.

Contact Tamara S. Estep, Director of Graduate Business Programs, Ball State University, College of

Ball State University

Business-WB 146, Muncie, IN 47306. *Telephone:* 765-285-1931. *Fax:* 765-285-8818. *E-mail:* bsumba@bsuvc. bsu.edu. *Web site:* http://www.bsu. edu/business/mba.

DEGREE & CERTIFICATE PROGRAMS

Master of Business Administration (MBA)

In the fall of 1997 there were 171 students enrolled in this program. In 1996–97, 45 degrees were earned at a distance through this program.

Geographic service area/restrictions Program is available at sites in Kentucky, New Jersey and Indiana.

Application requirements *Prior education:* Baccalaureate degree. *Other requirements:* GMAT, TOEFL (for international applicants), college transcripts, an application fee of $15, resume.

Completion requirements 36–54 credit hours. *Maximum time for completion:* six years.

INDIVIDUAL COURSE SUBJECT AREAS

Graduate

Accounting; Business Law; Economics; Finance; Management; Manufacturing Management; Marketing

BELLEVUE UNIVERSITY
College of Business
Bellevue, Nebraska

Bellevue University, founded in 1965, is an independent-nonprofit comprehensive institution. It is accredited by the North Central Association of Colleges and Schools. The College of Business first offered graduate business distance learning courses in 1997. In 1997–98, it offered 12 graduate business courses at a distance. In the fall of 1997, there were 33 students enrolled in distance learning graduate-level business courses and programs.

Course delivery sites Students can receive instruction anywhere.

Media Courses are delivered via audioconferencing, computer software, CD-ROM, computer conferencing, World Wide Web, e-mail, print. Students and teachers may interact via audioconferencing, mail, telephone, fax, e-mail, World Wide Web. The following equipment may be required: a computer with at least 4 MB of RAM, 4 MB of available hard drive space, a modem, and an Internet Service Provider.

Geographic service area/ restrictions Programs are available worldwide.

Services Distance learners have access to library services, academic advising, career placement assistance, bookstore at a distance.

Credit-earning options Students may transfer credits from another institution or may earn credits through military training, business training.

Typical costs Tuition of $275 per credit. Financial aid is available to distance learners.

Registration Students may register by mail, fax, e-mail, World Wide Web.

Contact Graduate Admissions, Bellevue University, 1000 Galvin Road, S, Bellevue, NE 68005. *Telephone:* 800-756-7920, Ext. 3702. *Fax:* 402-293-3730. *E-mail:* online_g@scholars. bellevue.edu. *Web site:* http://www. bellevue.edu.

DEGREE & CERTIFICATE PROGRAMS

Master of Business Administration (MBA)

In the fall of 1997 there were 30 students enrolled in this program.

Application requirements *Prior education:* an American undergraduate degree or the equivalent. *Other requirements:* GMAT, MAT, or GRE, college transcripts, an essay or personal statement, letter(s) of recommendation, an application fee of $50, work experience, minimum GPA of 2.5 for the previous 60 hours of credit and a cumulative GPA of 3.0 for prior graduate work.

Completion requirements 36 credits are required. *Maximum time for completion:* seven years.

BOWIE STATE UNIVERSITY

Department of Business and Economics

Bowie, Maryland

Bowie State University, founded in 1865, is a state-supported comprehensive institution. It is accredited by the Middle States Association of Colleges and Schools.

Course delivery sites Courses are delivered to 3 off-campus centers in Essex, Laurel, Reisterstown.

Media Courses are delivered via interactive television. Students and teachers may interact via fax, interactive television.

Geographic service area/restrictions Programs are available locally. Applicants must meet graduate admission requirements.

Services Distance learners have access to library services, the campus computer network, e-mail services, academic advising, tutoring, career placement assistance, bookstore at a distance.

Credit-earning options Students may transfer credits from another institution.

Typical costs Tuition of $158 per credit plus mandatory fees of $84.50 per semester for in-state residents. Tuition of $268 per credit plus mandatory fees of $84.50 per semester for out-of-state residents. Financial aid is available to distance learners.

Registration Students may register by mail, fax.

Contact Dr. Ida Brandon, Dean, School of Continuing Education, Bowie State University, 14000 Jericho Park Road, Bowie, MD 20715. *Telephone:* 301-464-6586. *Fax:* 301-464-7786. *E-mail:* ida.brandon@bowiestate.edu.

DEGREE & CERTIFICATE PROGRAMS

Master of Science (MS)

In the fall of 1997 there were 10 students enrolled in this program.

Application requirements *Prior education:* Baccalaureate degree in business management or information systems. *Other requirements:* college transcripts, an application fee of $35.

Completion requirements 36 semester hours are required. *Other requirements:* students must maintain a 3.5 GPA in the first 12 to 18 credits to advance to candidacy. *Maximum time for completion:* seven years.

On-campus requirements A comprehensive examination is administered on campus.

INDIVIDUAL COURSE SUBJECT AREAS

Graduate
Management; Management Information Systems; Public and Private Management

CALIFORNIA STATE UNIVERSITY, DOMINGUEZ HILLS

School of Management
Carson, California

California State University, Dominguez Hills, founded in 1960, is a state-supported comprehensive institution. It is accredited by the Western Association of Schools and Colleges, Inc. The School of Management first offered graduate business distance learning courses in 1997. In 1997–98, it offered 10 graduate business courses at a distance. In the fall of 1997, there were 50 students enrolled in distance learning graduate-level business courses and programs.

Course delivery sites Students can receive instruction anywhere.

Media Courses are delivered via videoconferencing, audioconferencing, computer software, CD-ROM, computer conferencing, World Wide Web, e-mail, print. Students and teachers may interact via videoconferencing, audioconferencing, e-mail, World Wide Web. The following equipment may be required: a Pentium computer.

Geographic service area/restrictions Programs are available worldwide. Students must meet the admissions standards for the MBA program.

Services Distance learners have access to library services, e-mail services, academic advising, bookstore at a distance.

Credit-earning options Students may transfer credits from another institution.

Typical costs Tuition of $800 per course. Financial aid is available to distance learners.

Registration Students may register by mail, fax, phone, e-mail, World Wide Web.

Contact Dr. David Karber, MBA ONLINE Coordinator, California State University, Dominguez Hills, School of Management, 1000 East Victoria Street, Carson, CA 90747. *Telephone:* 310-243-3661. *Fax:* 310-

217-6942. *E-mail:* dkarber@soma. csudh.edu. *Web site:* http://som.csudh. edu/internet.mba.

DEGREE & CERTIFICATE PROGRAMS

Master of Business Administration (MBA)
In the fall of 1997 there were 15 students enrolled in this program.

Application requirements *Prior education:* Baccalaureate degree. *Other requirements:* GMAT, college transcripts, an application fee of $55, minimum undergraduate GPA of 2.75.

Completion requirements 30 semester units. *Maximum time for completion:* five years.

CAMERON UNIVERSITY

School of Graduate and Professional Studies
Lawton, Oklahoma

Cameron University, founded in 1908, is a state-supported comprehensive institution. It is accredited by the North Central Association of Colleges and Schools. The School of Graduate and Professional Studies first offered graduate business distance learning courses in 1997. In 1997–98, it offered 22 graduate business courses at a distance.

Course delivery sites Courses are delivered to East Central University (Ada), University of Science and Arts of Oklahoma (Chickasha), Western Oklahoma State College (Altus), 1 off-campus center in Duncan.

Media Courses are delivered via interactive television. Students and teachers may meet in person or interact via mail, telephone, fax, e-mail, interactive television, World Wide Web.

Geographic service area/restrictions Programs are available statewide. Students must be admitted to the graduate school.

Services Distance learners have access to e-mail services, academic advising at a distance.

Credit-earning options Students may transfer credits from another institution.

Typical costs Tuition of $98 per credit hour for in-state residents. Tuition of $200 per credit hour for out-of-state residents. Financial aid is available to distance learners.

Registration Students may register by phone.

Contact Dr. David Carl, Dean, School of Graduate and Professional Studies, Cameron University, 2800 West Gore Boulevard, Lawton, OK 73505. *Telephone:* 580-581-2986. *Fax:* 580-581-5532. *E-mail:* graduate@cameron. edu. *Web site:* http://www.cameron. edu/academic/graduate/business/mba. html.

DEGREE & CERTIFICATE PROGRAMS

Master of Business Administration (MBA)

In the fall of 1997 there were 34 students enrolled in this program.

Application requirements *Prior education:* Baccalaureate degree. *Other requirements:* GMAT, college transcripts, an application fee of $15.

Completion requirements 33–45 semester credits. *Other requirements:* students must complete a comprehensive written exam. *Maximum time for completion:* five years.

INDIVIDUAL COURSE SUBJECT AREAS

Graduate
Accounting; Business Ethics; Economics; Finance; Management; Management Information Systems; Marketing; Organizational Management

Noncredit
Accounting; Business Ethics; Economics; Finance; Management; Management Information Systems; Marketing; Organizational Management

CARNEGIE MELLON UNIVERSITY

Graduate School of Industrial Administration
Pittsburgh, Pennsylvania

Carnegie Mellon University, founded in 1900, is an independent-nonprofit university. It is accredited by the Middle States Association of Colleges and Schools. The Graduate School of Industrial Administration first offered graduate business distance learning courses in 1996. In 1997–98, it offered 17 graduate business courses at a distance. In the fall of 1997, there were 42 students enrolled in distance learning graduate-level business courses and programs.

Course delivery sites Courses are delivered to corporate sponsor-chosen sites.

Media Courses are delivered via videoconferencing, interactive television, computer software, computer conferencing, World Wide Web, e-mail. Students and teachers may interact via mail, telephone, fax, e-mail, interactive television, World Wide Web. The following equipment may be required: a computer with PictureTel and access to the Internet.

Geographic service area/ restrictions Programs are available nationwide. Students must fulfill admissions requirements identical to the on-campus program and be enrolled in the program.

Services Distance learners have access to library services, the campus computer network, e-mail services, academic advising, tutoring at a distance.

Typical costs Tuition of $2040 per course.

Registration Students may register by fax, phone, e-mail.

Contact Dr. Nick Flor, Assistant Professor and Associate Director, Flex-Mode Program, Carnegie Mellon University, 5000 Forbes Avenue, Pittsburgh, PA 15213. *Telephone:* 412-268-5040. *Fax:* 412-268-7357. *E-mail:* flor@andrew.cmu.edu. *Web site:* http://www.gsia.cmu.edu.

DEGREE & CERTIFICATE PROGRAMS

Master of Science (MS)

In the fall of 1997 there were 42 students enrolled in this program.

Geographic service area/ restrictions Students must be the employees of corporate partners.

Application requirements *Prior education:* Baccalaureate degree. *Other requirements:* GMAT, college transcripts, an essay or personal statement, letter(s) of recommendation, an application fee of $60, work experience.

Completion requirements 204 units are required. *Maximum time for completion:* three years.

On-campus requirements Students must be on campus for orientation and graduation.

CITY UNIVERSITY
Bellevue, Washington

City University, founded in 1973, is an independent-nonprofit comprehensive institution. It is accredited by the Northwest Association of Schools and Colleges.

Course delivery sites Courses are delivered to your home, military bases.

Media Courses are delivered via videotapes, computer software, computer conferencing, World Wide Web, e-mail. Students and teachers may interact via mail, telephone, fax, e-mail, World Wide Web.

Geographic service area/restrictions Programs are available worldwide.

Typical costs Tuition of $280 per credit hour.

Contact Distance Learning Advisor, City University, Admissions and Student Affairs, 919 Southwest Grady Way, Renton, WA 98055. *Telephone:* 800-426-5596. *Fax:* 425-277-2437. *E-mail:* info@cityu.edu.

DEGREE & CERTIFICATE PROGRAMS

Executive Master of Arts (EMA)

Application requirements *Prior education:* Baccalaureate degree. *Other requirements:* an application fee of $75.

Completion requirements 45 credit hours are required.

Master of Business Administration (MBA)

Application requirements *Prior education:* Baccalaureate degree. *Other requirements:* an application fee of $75.

Completion requirements 45 credit hours are required.

Master of Public Administration (MPA)

Application requirements *Prior education:* Baccalaureate degree. *Other requirements:* an application fee of $75.

Completion requirements 45 credit hours are required.

Master of Science (MS)

Application requirements *Prior education:* Baccalaureate degree. *Other requirements:* an application fee of $75.

Completion requirements 45 credit hours are required.

Certificate

Application requirements *Prior education:* Baccalaureate degree. *Other requirements:* an application fee of $75.

Completion requirements 12–24 credit hours.

City University

INDIVIDUAL COURSE SUBJECT AREAS

Graduate
Finance; Management; Organizational
Behavior/Development

MBA–Distance Learning Programs

COLLEGE FOR FINANCIAL PLANNING

Denver, Colorado

College for Financial Planning is an independent-nonprofit graduate institution. It is accredited by the North Central Association of Colleges and Schools. It first offered graduate business distance learning courses in 1988. In 1997–98, it offered 17 graduate business courses at a distance.

Course delivery sites Students can receive instruction anywhere.

Media Courses are delivered via World Wide Web, e-mail, print. Students and teachers may interact via mail, telephone, fax, e-mail, World Wide Web. The following equipment may be required: a computer with access to the Internet.

Geographic service area/restrictions Programs are available nationwide. Students must have an undergraduate degree and a minimum GPA of 2.5 for graduate business courses.

Services Distance learners have access to library services, e-mail services at a distance.

Credit-earning options Students may transfer credits from another institution.

Typical costs Tuition of $600 per course. *Non-credit courses:* $525 per course.

Registration Students may register by mail, phone.

Contact Glen Steelman, Registrar, College for Financial Planning, 4695 South Monaco Street, Denver, CO 80237. *Telephone:* 303-220-4861. *Fax:* 303-220-4941. *Web site:* http://www.fp.edu.

DEGREE & CERTIFICATE PROGRAMS

Master of Science (MS)

In 1996–97, 57 degrees were earned at a distance through this program.

Application requirements *Prior education:* Baccalaureate degree in a business-related subject. *Other requirements:* college transcripts, an application fee of $225, work experience.

Completion requirements 36 credit hours are required. *Other requirements:* students are required to complete a research paper involving computer applications at the end of the program. *Maximum time for completion:* seven years.

COLLEGE OF INSURANCE
Center for Professional Education
New York, New York

College of Insurance, founded in 1962, is an independent-nonprofit comprehensive institution. It is accredited by the Middle States Association of Colleges and Schools. The Center for Professional Education first offered graduate business distance learning courses in 1996. In 1997–98, it offered 4 graduate business courses at a distance. In the fall of 1997, there were 12 students enrolled in distance learning graduate-level business courses and programs.

Course delivery sites Courses are delivered to The Bermuda Insurance Institute (Hamilton, Bermuda).

Media Courses are delivered via e-mail, visiting faculty. Students and teachers may meet in person or interact via mail, fax, e-mail, World Wide Web. The following equipment may be required: a computer.

Geographic service area/ restrictions Programs are limited to site in Hamilton, Bermuda. Applicants must meet admission requirements.

Services Distance learners have access to library services, e-mail services, academic advising, tutoring, career placement assistance at a distance.

Credit-earning options Students may transfer credits from another institution.

Typical costs Tuition of $535 per credit plus mandatory fees of $15 per credit.

Registration Students may register by mail, fax.

Contact Theresa Marro, Director of Admissions, College of Insurance, 101 Murray Street, New York, NY 10007-2165. *Telephone:* 212-815-9232. *Fax:* 212-964-3381. *E-mail:* tmarro@tcl.edu.

DEGREE & CERTIFICATE PROGRAMS

Master of Business Administration (MBA)

In the fall of 1997 there were 12 students enrolled in this program.

Geographic service area/ restrictions Program is available in Hamilton, Bermuda.

Application requirements *Prior education:* Baccalaureate degree. *Other requirements:* GMAT, college transcripts, an essay or personal statement, letter(s) of recommendation, an application fee of $25, work experience.

Completion requirements 51 credits are required.

Graduate

Insurance; Risk Management

COLLEGE OF ST. SCHOLASTICA

Duluth, Minnesota

College of St. Scholastica, founded in 1912, is an independent-religious comprehensive institution affiliated with the Roman Catholic Church. It is accredited by the North Central Association of Colleges and Schools. It first offered graduate business distance learning courses in 1990. In 1997–98, it offered 6 graduate business courses at a distance. In the fall of 1997, there were 17 students enrolled in distance learning graduate-level business courses and programs.

Course delivery sites Students can receive instruction anywhere.

Media Courses are delivered via videotapes, interactive television, print, intensive summer sessions on campus. Students and teachers may meet in person or interact via audioconferencing, mail, telephone, fax, e-mail, interactive television. The following equipment may be required: a TV and a VCR for videotape-based courses.

Geographic service area/restrictions Programs are available regionally.

Services Distance learners have access to library services, the campus computer network, e-mail services, academic advising, bookstore at a distance.

Credit-earning options Students may transfer credits from another institution.

Typical costs Tuition of $332 per quarter credit. Financial aid is available to distance learners.

Registration Students may register by mail, fax.

Contact Pat Jones, Management Department Coordinator, College of St. Scholastica, 1200 Kenwood Avenue, Duluth, MN 55811. *Telephone:* 218-723-6415. *Fax:* 218-723-6290. *E-mail:* pjones@css.edu. *Web site:* http://www.css.edu.

DEGREE & CERTIFICATE PROGRAMS

Master of Arts (MA)

In the fall of 1997 there were 17 students enrolled in this program.

Geographic service area/restrictions Program is available in regional area only.

Application requirements *Prior education:* Baccalaureate degree. *Other requirements:* college transcripts, an essay or personal statement, an application fee of $50, work experience, phone interview.

Completion requirements 50–53 quarter credits. *Maximum time for completion:* seven years.

On-campus requirements Students must attend two-week summer sessions.

INDIVIDUAL COURSE SUBJECT AREAS

Graduate
Finance; Operations Management

COLORADO STATE UNIVERSITY

Distance Degree Program

Fort Collins, Colorado

Colorado State University, founded in 1870, is a state-supported university. It is accredited by the North Central Association of Colleges and Schools. The Distance Degree Program first offered graduate business distance learning courses in 1967. In 1997–98, it offered 211 graduate business courses at a distance. In the fall of 1997, there were 646 students enrolled in distance learning graduate-level business courses and programs.

Course delivery sites Students can receive instruction anywhere.

Media Courses are delivered via videotapes, computer software, computer conferencing, World Wide Web, e-mail, print. Students and teachers may interact via mail, telephone, fax, e-mail. The following equipment may be required: a TV and a VCR and/or a computer with email.

Geographic service area/ restrictions Programs are available in the United States and Canada. Students must fulfill specific prerequisites.

Services Distance learners have access to library services, e-mail services, academic advising at a distance.

Credit-earning options Students may transfer credits from another institution.

Typical costs Students pay from $312–$364 per credit depending on where the tapes are delivered. Financial aid is available to distance learners.

Registration Students may register by mail, fax.

Contact Distance Degree Program, Colorado State University, Division of Educational Outreach, Spruce Hall, Fort Collins, CO 80523-1040. *Telephone:* 970-491-5288. *Fax:* 970-491-7885. *E-mail:* info@learn.colostate. edu. *Web site:* http://www.colostate. edu/depts/CE.

DEGREE & CERTIFICATE PROGRAMS

Master of Business Administration (MBA)

In the fall of 1997 there were 473 students enrolled in this program. In 1996–97, 70 degrees were earned at a distance through this program.

Geographic service area/ restrictions Program is available in the United States and Canada.

Application requirements *Prior education:* Baccalaureate degree. *Other*
requirements: GMAT, college transcripts, an application fee of $30, work experience.

Completion requirements 36 semester credits are required. *Maximum time for completion:* ten years.

INDIVIDUAL COURSE SUBJECT AREAS

Graduate

Accounting; Finance; Management; Marketing

DRAKE UNIVERSITY
College of Business and Public Administration
Des Moines, Iowa

Drake University, founded in 1881, is an independent-nonprofit university. It is accredited by the North Central Association of Colleges and Schools. The College of Business and Public Administration first offered graduate business distance learning courses in 1994. In 1997–98, it offered 6 graduate business courses at a distance. In the fall of 1997, there were 23 students enrolled in distance learning graduate-level business courses and programs.

Course delivery sites Courses are delivered to Iowa Lakes Community College (Estherville), North Iowa Area Community College (Mason City), Southwestern Community College (Creston).

Media Courses are delivered via interactive television, World Wide Web, e-mail, print. Students and teachers may meet in person or interact via mail, telephone, fax, e-mail, interactive television, World Wide Web.

Geographic service area/ restrictions Programs are available statewide. Students must be admitted to a Master's degree granting program or already hold a Master's degree or higher.

Services Distance learners have access to library services, the campus computer network, e-mail services, academic advising, career placement assistance, bookstore at a distance.

Credit-earning options Students may transfer credits from another institution.

Typical costs Tuition of $340 per hour. Financial aid is available to distance learners.

Registration Students may register by mail, phone.

Contact Dr. Thomas M. Pursel, Director of Graduate Programs, Drake University, College of Business and Public Administration, Des Moines, IA 50311. *Telephone:* 515-271-2188. *Fax:* 515-271-4518.

DEGREE & CERTIFICATE PROGRAMS

Master of Business Administration (MBA)

In the fall of 1997 there were 23 students enrolled in this program.

Application requirements *Prior education:* Baccalaureate degree. *Other*

requirements: GMAT, college transcripts, an application fee of $25.

Completion requirements 36 semester hours are required. *Maximum time for completion:* five years.

DUKE UNIVERSITY
Fuqua School of Business–Executive MBA Programs
Durham, North Carolina

Duke University, founded in 1838, is an independent-religious university affiliated with the United Methodist Church. It is accredited by the Southern Association of Colleges and Schools. The Fuqua School of Business first offered graduate business distance learning courses in 1996. In 1997–98, it offered 15 graduate business courses at a distance.

Course delivery sites Courses are delivered to your home, 6 off-campus centers in Buenos Aires (Argentina), Sao Paolo (Brazil), Hong Kong (China), Shanghai (China), Prague (Czech Republic), Salzburg (Austria).

Media Courses are delivered via videotapes, videoconferencing, computer software, CD-ROM, computer conferencing, World Wide Web, e-mail, print. Students and teachers may meet in person or interact via mail, telephone, fax, e-mail, World Wide Web. The following equipment may be required: a laptop computer with the related software.

Geographic service area/ restrictions Programs are available worldwide.

Services Distance learners have access to library services, the campus computer network, e-mail services at a distance.

Typical costs Tuition of $82,500 per degree program.

Contact Sam Veraldi, Assistant Dean of Admissions, Duke University, Fuqua School of Business, PO Box 90127, Durham, NC 27708. *Telephone:* 919-660-7802. *Fax:* 919-660-8044. *E-mail:* veraldi@mail.duke.edu.

DEGREE & CERTIFICATE PROGRAMS

Executive Master of Business Administration (EMBA)

In 1996–97, 39 degrees were earned at a distance through this program.

Application requirements *Prior education:* Baccalaureate degree. *Other requirements:* TOEFL (for international applicants), college transcripts, an essay or personal statement, letter(s) of recommendation, an application fee, work experience.

Completion requirements 15 courses are required. *Maximum time for completion:* nineteen months.

On-campus requirements Students must complete one two-week and one three-week residency.

DUQUESNE UNIVERSITY
Graduate School of Business
Pittsburgh, Pennsylvania

Duquesne University, founded in 1878, is an independent-religious Roman Catholic university. It is accredited by the Middle States Association of Colleges and Schools.

Course delivery sites Students can receive instruction anywhere.

Media Courses are delivered via television, videoconferencing, audioconferencing, computer software, CD-ROM, computer conferencing, World Wide Web, e-mail. Students and teachers may meet in person or interact via videoconferencing, mail, telephone, fax, e-mail, World Wide Web. The following equipment may be required: a computer with a 28.8K or faster modem, a web browser, and Windows 95.

Geographic service area/ restrictions Programs are available worldwide.

Services Distance learners have access to library services, the campus computer network, e-mail services, academic advising, career placement assistance, bookstore at a distance.

Credit-earning options Students may transfer credits from another institution or may earn credits through examinations.

Typical costs Tuition of $481 per credit plus mandatory fees of $39 per credit. *Non-credit courses:* $50–$100. Financial aid is available to distance learners.

Registration Students may register by mail, fax, phone, e-mail, World Wide Web.

Contact Graduate Business Office, Duquesne University, 704 Rockwell Hall, Pittsburgh, PA 15282. *Telephone:* 412-396-6276. *Fax:* 412-396-5034. *Web site:* http://www.bus.duq.edu.

INDIVIDUAL COURSE SUBJECT AREAS

Noncredit
Business Information Science; Finance; Human Resources; Leadership; Marketing; Strategic Management; Technology Management

EASTERN COLLEGE

Business Department
St. Davids, Pennsylvania

Eastern College, founded in 1952, is an independent-religious American Baptist comprehensive institution. It is accredited by the Middle States Association of Colleges and Schools. The Business Department first offered graduate business distance learning courses in 1997. In 1997–98, it offered 15 graduate business courses at a distance. In the fall of 1997, there were 3 students enrolled in distance learning graduate-level business courses and programs.

Course delivery sites Students can receive instruction anywhere.

Media Courses are delivered via videotapes. Students and teachers may meet in person or interact via mail, telephone, fax, e-mail, World Wide Web. The following equipment may be required: a TV and a VCR.

Geographic service area/restrictions Programs are available worldwide.

Services Distance learners have access to library services, e-mail services, bookstore at a distance.

Credit-earning options Students may transfer credits from another institution or may earn credits through examinations.

Typical costs Tuition of $368 per credit plus mandatory fees of $100 per course. Students may register for undergraduate foundation courses at a cost of $305 per credit. Financial aid is available to distance learners.

Registration Students may register by mail, fax, phone.

Contact Megan Miscioscia, Graduate Admissions Representative, Eastern College, 1300 Eagle Road, St. Davids, PA 19087-3696. *Telephone:* 610-341-5972. *Fax:* 610-341-1466. *E-mail:* gradadm@eastern.edu.

INDIVIDUAL COURSE SUBJECT AREAS

Graduate
Developmental Economics; Economics; Finance; Management; Strategic Management

EASTERN NEW MEXICO UNIVERSITY

College of Business
Portales, New Mexico

Eastern New Mexico University, founded in 1934, is a state-supported comprehensive institution. It is accredited by the North Central Association of Colleges and Schools. The College of Business first offered graduate business distance learning courses in 1980. In 1997–98, it offered 8 graduate business courses at a distance. In the fall of 1997, there were 30 students enrolled in distance learning graduate-level business courses and programs.

Course delivery sites Courses are delivered to military bases, high schools, Clovis Community College (Clovis), Eastern New Mexico University–Roswell (Roswell), New Mexico Junior College (Hobbs).

Media Courses are delivered via interactive television. Students and teachers may meet in person or interact via fax, e-mail, interactive television, World Wide Web.

Geographic service area/restrictions Programs are available in eastern New Mexico.

Services Distance learners have access to library services, the campus computer network, e-mail services, academic advising, bookstore at a distance.

Credit-earning options Students may transfer credits from another institu-tion or may earn credits through examinations.

Typical costs Tuition of $103 per credit for in-state residents. Tuition of $266 per credit for out-of-state residents. Financial aid is available to distance learners.

Registration Students may register by mail, fax, phone, e-mail.

Contact Dr. Gerry Huybregts, Interim Dean, Eastern New Mexico University, College of Business, Station 49, Portales, NM 88130. *Telephone:* 505-562-2737. *Fax:* 505-562-4331. *E-mail:* gerry.huybregts@enmu.edu. *Web site:* http://www.enmu.edu.

DEGREE & CERTIFICATE PROGRAMS

Master of Business Administration (MBA)

In the fall of 1997 there were 44 students enrolled in this program. In 1996–97, 5 degrees were earned at a distance through this program.

Geographic service area/ restrictions Program is available in eastern New Mexico.

Application requirements *Prior education:* Baccalaureate degree. *Other requirements:* GMAT, college transcripts, an application fee of $10, work experience.

Completion requirements 33 semester units. *Maximum time for completion:* six years.

On-campus requirements Students are required to be on campus twice per semester.

INDIVIDUAL COURSE SUBJECT AREAS

Graduate
Accounting; Business Policy/Strategy; Economics; Finance; Marketing; Operations Management; Organizational Behavior/Development

EAST TENNESSEE STATE UNIVERSITY

Johnson City, Tennessee

East Tennessee State University, founded in 1911, is a state-supported university. It is accredited by the Southern Association of Colleges and Schools. It first offered graduate business distance learning courses in 1990.

Course delivery sites Courses are delivered to 3 off-campus centers in Bristol, Greeneville, Kingsport.

Media Courses are delivered via television, interactive television. Students and teachers may meet in person or interact via mail, telephone, fax, e-mail, interactive television.

Geographic service area/restrictions Programs are available locally. Students must be admitted to the graduate school to take credit courses.

Services Distance learners have access to library services, the campus computer network, e-mail services, bookstore at a distance.

Credit-earning options Students may transfer credits from another institution.

Typical costs Tuition of $126 per semester hour plus mandatory fees of $15 per semester hour for in-state residents. Tuition of $327 per semester hour plus mandatory fees of $15 per semester hour for out-of-state residents. Financial aid is available to distance learners.

Registration Students may register by phone.

Contact Dr. Ron Green, Associate Dean, East Tennessee State University, College of Business, Box 70699, Johnson City, TN 37614. *Telephone:* 423-439-5314. *E-mail:* greenr@etsu.edu. *Web site:* http://www.etsu.edu/scs/distedu.htm.

DEGREE & CERTIFICATE PROGRAMS

Master of Business Administration (MBA)

Geographic service area/restrictions Students must participate in cohort groups.

Application requirements *Prior education:* Baccalaureate degree. *Other requirements:* GMAT, college transcripts, an essay or personal statement, an application fee of $25–$35, work experience.

Completion requirements 39 semester hours are required. *Maximum time for completion:* six years.

INDIVIDUAL COURSE SUBJECT AREAS

Graduate
Management; Marketing

EDITH COWAN UNIVERSITY

Business Faculty
Churchlands, Australia

Edith Cowan University is a university in Australia. The Business Faculty first offered graduate business distance learning courses in 1972. In 1997–98, it offered 3 graduate business courses at a distance. In the fall of 1997, there were 157 students enrolled in distance learning graduate-level business courses and programs.

Course delivery sites Students can receive instruction anywhere.

Media Courses are delivered via videotapes, audiotapes, computer software, CD-ROM, World Wide Web, e-mail, print. Students and teachers may meet in person or interact via mail, telephone, fax, e-mail, World Wide Web. The following equipment may be required: a computer.

Geographic service area/restrictions Programs are available worldwide.

Services Distance learners have access to library services, the campus computer network, e-mail services, academic advising, tutoring, career placement assistance, bookstore at a distance.

Credit-earning options Students may transfer credits from another institution or may earn credits through portfolio assessment.

Typical costs Tuition of $900 per unit. *Non-credit courses:* $900 per unit.

Registration Students may register by mail, fax, World Wide Web.

Contact Ully Walter, Admissions Coordinator, Edith Cowan University, External Studies, PO Box 830, Claremont, West Australia 6010, Australia. *Telephone:* 61-894421460. *E-mail:* u.walter@cowan.edu.au.

DEGREE & CERTIFICATE PROGRAMS

Master of Business Administration (MBA)

In the fall of 1997 there were 41 students enrolled in this program. In 1996–97, 17 degrees were earned at a distance through this program.

Application requirements *Prior education:* Graduate degree. *Other requirements:* college transcripts, letter(s) of recommendation, work experience, application form (no charge).

INDIVIDUAL COURSE SUBJECT AREAS

Graduate
Management; Management Information Systems

Noncredit
Management; Management Information Systems

GOLDEN GATE UNIVERSITY

Cyber Campus

San Francisco, California

Golden Gate University, founded in 1853, is an independent-nonprofit university. It is accredited by the Western Association of Schools and Colleges, Inc. The Cyber Campus first offered graduate business distance learning courses in 1997. In 1997–98, it offered 11 graduate business courses at a distance. In the fall of 1997, there were 268 students enrolled in distance learning graduate-level business courses and programs.

Course delivery sites Students can receive instruction anywhere.

Media Courses are delivered via computer conferencing, World Wide Web. Students and teachers may interact via mail, telephone, fax, e-mail, World Wide Web. The following equipment may be required: a computer with a modem (14.4K or better) and a web browser.

Geographic service area/restrictions Programs are available worldwide.

Services Distance learners have access to library services, the campus computer network, e-mail services, academic advising, career placement assistance, bookstore at a distance.

Typical costs Students pay $996–$1,494 per course. Tuition is for 1998–99. Costs may vary by specific program of study. Financial aid is available to distance learners.

Registration Students may register by mail, World Wide Web.

Contact Sonali Sahni, Academic Coordinator, Golden Gate University, 536 Mission Street, San Francisco, CA 94105. *Telephone:* 415-442-7060. *Fax:* 415-896-2394. *E-mail:* ssahni@ggu.edu. *Web site:* http://cybercampus.ggu.edu.

DEGREE & CERTIFICATE PROGRAMS

Certificate in Healthcare Management

Application requirements *Prior education:* Baccalaureate degree. *Other requirements:* college transcripts, an application fee of $55.

Completion requirements 18 units are required.

INDIVIDUAL COURSE SUBJECT AREAS

Graduate
Arts Administration/Management; Finance; Management; Management Information Systems; Marketing; Organizational Behavior/Development; Taxation

HERIOT-WATT UNIVERSITY

Edinburgh, United Kingdom

Heriot-Watt University is a university in the United Kingdom. It first offered graduate business distance learning courses in 1990.

Course delivery sites Students can receive instruction anywhere.

Media Courses are delivered via computer software, print. Students and teachers may interact via mail, fax, e-mail.

Geographic service area/restrictions Programs are available worldwide. The program has open access but students without prior qualifications must pass two core courses before being able to register as a matriculated student.

Services Distance learners have access to e-mail services, academic advising at a distance.

Credit-earning options Students may earn credits through examinations.

Typical costs Mandatory fees of $720 per course for in-state residents.

Registration Students may register by mail.

Contact Alick Kitchin, Development Manager, Heriot-Watt University, Financial Times Management, 128 Longacre, London, WC2 E9A, England. *Telephone:* 44-1713797383. *E-mail:* hwattmba@ftmanagement. com. *Web site:* http://www.ebs.hw.ac. uk.

DEGREE & CERTIFICATE PROGRAMS

Master of Business Administration (MBA)

In 1996–97, 450 degrees were earned at a distance through this program.

Application requirements £455 application fee.

Completion requirements 9 courses are required. *Other requirements:* testing is administered at over 300 examination centers worldwide. *Maximum time for completion:* seven years.

INDIVIDUAL COURSE SUBJECT AREAS

Graduate
Accounting; Economics; Finance; Marketing; Organizational Behavior/ Development; Quantitative Analysis; Strategic Management

ISIM UNIVERSITY

Denver, Colorado

ISIM University is an independent-nonprofit graduate institution. It is accredited by the Distance Education and Training Council. It first offered graduate business distance learning courses in 1994. In 1997–98, it offered 26 graduate business courses at a distance. In the fall of 1997, there were 124 students enrolled in distance learning graduate-level business courses and programs.

Course delivery sites Courses are delivered to your home, your workplace.

Media Courses are delivered via World Wide Web, e-mail, print. Students and teachers may interact via mail, telephone, fax, e-mail, World Wide Web. The following equipment may be required: a computer with access to the Internet.

Geographic service area/restrictions Programs are available worldwide. Applicants must meet admission requirements.

Services Distance learners have access to e-mail services, academic advising at a distance.

Credit-earning options Students may transfer credits from another institution or may earn credits through examinations, portfolio assessment.

Typical costs Tuition of $1125 per course. Costs may vary by campus or location, number of credits taken.

Registration Students may register by mail, fax, e-mail.

Contact Robin Thompson, Admissions Representative, ISIM University, 501 South Cherry Street, Denver, CO 80246. *Telephone:* 303-333-4224. *Fax:* 303-336-1144. *E-mail:* admissions@ isimu.edu.

DEGREE & CERTIFICATE PROGRAMS

Master of Business Administration (MBA)

Application requirements *Prior education:* Baccalaureate degree. *Other requirements:* college transcripts, an essay or personal statement, letter(s) of recommendation, an application fee of $50, work experience.

Completion requirements 36 units are required.

Master of Science (MS)

Application requirements *Prior education:* Baccalaureate degree. *Other requirements:* college transcripts, an essay or personal statement, letter(s) of recommendation, an application fee of $50, work experience.

Completion requirements 36 units are required.

INDIVIDUAL COURSE SUBJECT AREAS

Graduate
Management; Management Information Systems

ISIM UNIVERSITY

International School of Information Management

Denver, Colorado

THE COLLEGE

Founded in 1987, ISIM University serves both individuals and organizations by providing its distance education offerings worldwide. ISIM is accredited by the Distance Education and Training Council in Washington, D.C., and recognized by the Colorado Commission of Higher Education to offer graduate degree programs, executive education, and continuing education. ISIM University is also a member of the United States Distance Learning Association.

DISTANCE LEARNING PROGRAM

ISIM University offers graduate degrees in business administration and information management to students worldwide with an eye on the global marketplace. Within the two graduate degree programs offered, ISIM University provides opportunities for independent study for individuals who wish to focus on a specific field of study. In addition to graduate programs, ISIM offers classes for executive education in finance, project management, C Intranet technology, and other career-enhancing courses for the professional adult.

DELIVERY MEDIA

ISIM University's programs are offered through the Internet and are accessible via any Web browser. Individuals who have Internet access can log onto ISIM's electronic classroom. In addition, ISIM University offers its curriculum through its guided self-study approach, in which individuals with limited Internet access may study on their own. ISIM University has no residence requirement; students communicate and exchange information with their instructors and each other through the electronic classroom, e-mail, the postal service, facsimile, or telephone. The ISIM approach to education is flexible, allowing the student to study on his or her own time from anywhere in the world.

SPECIAL PROGRAMS

ISIM University provides additional programs for individuals who wish to increase their knowledge. These programs cover subjects such as project management, strategic management, and Intranets. ISIM has also designed programs for corporations and organizations that have diverse employee populations and want to save money on travel.

FACULTY

ISIM University's faculty is made up of full-time educators as well as industry experts and business professionals who teach part-time for the University. All faculty members have advanced degrees, and most have terminal degrees within their disciplines.

CREDIT OPTIONS

Students have various options to enhance their learning background. These options include graduate transfer credit, credit by exam, portfolio-assisted assessments (experiential learning), and independent study.

ADMISSION

The principal requirement for admission into ISIM University is an undergraduate degree; however, ISIM does offer an executive-level M.B.A. program for individuals who do not have a bachelor's degree. ISIM does not require the GMAT or other graduate admission examinations.

TUITION AND FEES

ISIM tuition is $375 per credit hour for either the online program or the guided self-study program. Mailing costs and book costs are the responsibility of the student.

FINANCIAL AID

ISIM University does not participate in any government-funded financial aid programs. ISIM is eligible for tuition reimbursement by many corporations. ISIM University has flexible payment options, and students may apply for financial assistance with an independent educational financing agency.

APPLYING

Applications are accepted on an ongoing basis, with classes starting every ten weeks. There is a $50 nonrefundable application fee. Students must submit an application, the application fee, a current resume, college transcripts, three letters of recommendation, and a goal statement.

CONTACT

Tim Adams, Director of
   Admissions
Admissions Office, Room 350
501 South Cherry Street
Denver, Colorado 80246
Telephone: 303-333-4224
               800-441-ISIM (toll-
               free)
Fax: 303-336-1144
E-mail: admissions@isimu.edu
Web site: http://www.isimu.edu

KETTERING UNIVERSITY
Office of Graduate Studies
Flint, Michigan

Kettering University, founded in 1919, is an independent-nonprofit comprehensive institution. It is accredited by the North Central Association of Colleges and Schools. The Office of Graduate Studies first offered graduate business distance learning courses in 1982. In 1997–98, it offered 18 graduate business courses at a distance. In the fall of 1997, there were 670 students enrolled in distance learning graduate-level business courses and programs.

Course delivery sites Courses are delivered to your workplace, 116 off-campus centers.

Media Courses are delivered via videotapes. Students and teachers may meet in person or interact via mail, telephone, fax, e-mail.

Geographic service area/restrictions Programs are available nationwide.

Services Distance learners have access to library services, academic advising at a distance.

Credit-earning options Students may transfer credits from another institution.

Typical costs Tuition of $1185 per course plus mandatory fees of $45 per course. Financial aid is available to distance learners.

Registration Students may register by mail, fax.

Contact Betty Bedore, Coordinator of Publicity, Kettering University, 1700 West Third Avenue, Flint, MI 48504-4898. *Telephone:* 810-762-7494. *Fax:* 810-762-9935. *E-mail:* bbedore@kettering.edu. *Web site:* http://www.gmi.edu/official/acad/grad/.

DEGREE & CERTIFICATE PROGRAMS

Master of Science (MS)

In the fall of 1997 there were 670 students enrolled in this program. In 1996–97, 119 degrees were earned at a distance through this program.

Application requirements *Prior education:* Baccalaureate degree. *Other requirements:* GMAT, college transcripts, an essay or personal statement, letter(s) of recommendation.

Completion requirements 54 credits are required. *Maximum time for completion:* six years.

INDIVIDUAL COURSE SUBJECT AREAS

Graduate
Manufacturing Management

LAKE SUPERIOR STATE UNIVERSITY

School of Business

Sault Sainte Marie, Michigan

Lake Superior State University, founded in 1946, is a state-supported comprehensive institution. It is accredited by the North Central Association of Colleges and Schools. The School of Business first offered graduate business distance learning courses in 1988. In 1997–98, it offered 9 graduate business courses at a distance. In the fall of 1997, there were 30 students enrolled in distance learning graduate-level business courses and programs.

Course delivery sites Courses are delivered to Alpena Community College (Alpena), Bay de Noc Community College (Escanaba), North Central Michigan College (Petoskey), Northwestern Michigan College (Traverse City).

Media Courses are delivered via interactive television. Students and teachers may meet in person or interact via mail, telephone, fax, e-mail, interactive television.

Geographic service area/ restrictions Programs are available statewide.

Services Distance learners have access to library services, academic advising, bookstore at a distance.

Credit-earning options Students may transfer credits from another institution.

Typical costs Tuition of $168 per credit hour. *Non-credit courses:* $252 per course. Financial aid is available to distance learners.

Registration Students may register by mail, fax, phone.

Contact Susan K. Camp, Director of Continuing Education, Lake Superior State University, 650 West Easterday, Sault Sainte Marie, MI 49783. *Telephone:* 888-800-LSSU, Ext. 2554. *Fax:* 906-635-2762. *E-mail:* scamp@lakers.lssu.edu. *Web site:* http://www.lssu.edu.

DEGREE & CERTIFICATE PROGRAMS

Master of Business Administration (MBA)

In the fall of 1997 there were 30 students enrolled in this program.

Lake Superior State University

Application requirements *Prior education:* Baccalaureate degree in business. *Other requirements:* GMAT, college transcripts, letter(s) of recommendation, an application fee of $25.

Completion requirements 36 semester hours are required. *Maximum time for completion:* eight years.

INDIVIDUAL COURSE SUBJECT AREAS

Graduate

Advertising; Business Communications; Business Policy/Strategy; Finance; International Business; Management; Management Information Systems; Public Management

LEHIGH UNIVERSITY

MBA Program

Bethlehem, Pennsylvania

Lehigh University, founded in 1865, is an independent-nonprofit university. It is accredited by the Middle States Association of Colleges and Schools. The MBA Program first offered graduate business distance learning courses in 1994. In 1997–98, it offered 15 graduate business courses at a distance. In the fall of 1997, there were 106 students enrolled in distance learning graduate-level business courses and programs.

Course delivery sites Courses are delivered to your workplace.

Media Courses are delivered via televison. Students and teachers may interact via videoconferencing, audioconferencing, telephone, fax, e-mail, interactive television, World Wide Web. The following equipment may be required: a TV and VCR, a speakerphone, and/or a computer. Equipment requirements are met by the corporate sponsors.

Geographic service area/restrictions Programs are available nationwide. Students must be employees of corporate partners.

Services Distance learners have access to library services, the campus computer network, e-mail services, academic advising, bookstore at a distance.

Credit-earning options Students may transfer credits from another institution.

Typical costs Tuition of $555 per credit. *Non-credit courses:* $570 per course. Costs may vary by specific program of study.

Registration Students may register by mail, fax, phone.

Contact Kathleen A. Trexler, Associate Dean and Director, MBA Program, Lehigh University, Rauch Business Center, Room 195, 621 Taylor Street, Bethlehem, PA 18015. *Telephone:* 610-758-3418. *Fax:* 610-758-5283. *E-mail:* kat3@lehigh.edu. *Web site:* http://www.lehigh.edu/~incbe/incbe.html.

DEGREE & CERTIFICATE PROGRAMS

Master of Business Administration (MBA)

In the fall of 1997 there were 106 students enrolled in this program. In 1996–97, 11 degrees were earned at a distance through this program.

Geographic service area/ restrictions Students must be the employees of corporate partners.

Application requirements *Prior education:* Baccalaureate degree. *Other requirements:* GMAT, college transcripts, an essay or personal statement, letter(s) of recommendation, an application fee of $40.

Completion requirements 36 credit hours are required. *Maximum time for completion:* six years.

On-campus requirements Students must attend campus on two Saturdays during the duration of the program.

INDIVIDUAL COURSE SUBJECT AREAS

Graduate
Accounting; Advertising; Business Information Science; Business Law; Decision Sciences; Economics; Finance; Management; Management Information Systems

Noncredit
Accounting; Advertising; Business Information Science; Business Law; Decision Sciences; Economics; Finance; Management; Management Information Systems

LESLEY COLLEGE
School of Management
Cambridge, Massachusetts

Lesley College, founded in 1909, is an independent-nonprofit comprehensive institution. It is accredited by the New England Association of Schools and Colleges. The School of Management first offered graduate business distance learning courses in 1996. In 1997–98, it offered 1 graduate business course at a distance. In the fall of 1997, there were 10 students enrolled in distance learning graduate-level business courses and programs.

Course delivery sites Students can receive instruction anywhere.

Media Courses are delivered via interactive television, World Wide Web. Students and teachers may interact via mail, telephone, fax, e-mail, interactive television, World Wide Web. The following equipment may be required: a computer with access to the Internet and/or access to a corporate site capable of receiving or transmitting through video and phonelines.

Geographic service area/restrictions Programs are available worldwide. Video transmission courses require special arrangements with specific employers.

Services Distance learners have access to library services, academic advising, tutoring, bookstore at a distance.

Credit-earning options Students may transfer credits from another institution.

Typical costs Contact school for information.

Registration Students may register by mail, fax, phone, e-mail, World Wide Web.

Contact Prof. Richard Jette, Director of the Master of Science in Training and Development Program, Lesley College, 29 Everett Street, Cambridge, MA 02138. *Telephone:* 617-349-8656. *Fax:* 617-349-8678. *E-mail:* rjette@ lesley.edu. *Web site:* http://www. lesley.edu/som.html.

DEGREE & CERTIFICATE PROGRAMS

Master of Science (MS)

Geographic service area/restrictions Students must be the employees of corporate partners.

Application requirements *Prior education:* Baccalaureate degree. *Other requirements:* college transcripts, an essay or personal statement, letter(s) of recommendation, an application fee of $45, work experience, resume.

Completion requirements 36 semester credits are required. *Maximum time for completion:* seven years.

INDIVIDUAL COURSE SUBJECT AREAS

Graduate

Business Ethics; Human Resources

MADONNA UNIVERSITY
School of Business
Livonia, Michigan

Madonna University, founded in 1947, is an independent-religious Roman Catholic comprehensive institution. It is accredited by the North Central Association of Colleges and Schools. The School of Business first offered graduate business distance learning courses in 1989. In 1997–98, it offered 10 graduate business courses at a distance.

Course delivery sites Students can receive instruction anywhere.

Media Courses are delivered via videotapes, audiotapes, computer conferencing, World Wide Web, e-mail. Students and teachers may interact via fax, e-mail, World Wide Web. The following equipment may be required: a computer with a modem, an Internet Service Provider, and a web browser.

Geographic service area/ restrictions Programs are available worldwide. Students must be able to understand, read, and write the English language.

Services Distance learners have access to library services, the campus computer network, academic advising, bookstore at a distance.

Credit-earning options Students may transfer credits from another institution or may earn credits through military training, business training.

Typical costs Tuition of $9000 per degree program. Financial aid is available to distance learners.

Registration Students may register by mail, fax.

Contact Dr. C. L. Neuhauser, Director, Cohort Online Programs, Madonna University, School of Business, 36600 Schoolcraft Road, Livonia, MI 48150. *Telephone:* 734-432-5354. *Fax:* 734-492-5364. *E-mail:* neuhause@ smpt.munet.edu. *Web site:* http:// www.munet.edu.

DEGREE & CERTIFICATE PROGRAMS

Master of Science in Business Administration (MSBA)

Geographic service area/ restrictions Cohort program enrollment is limited to 25 students.

Application requirements *Prior education:* Baccalaureate degree. *Other requirements:* GMAT (if GPA is under 3.25), college transcripts, an essay or personal statement, letter(s) of recommendation, work experience.

Completion requirements 36 semester hours are required. *Maximum time for completion: 22 months.*

INDIVIDUAL COURSE SUBJECT AREAS

Graduate

Accounting; Management Information Systems; Organizational Behavior/ Development; Strategic Management

MAHARISHI UNIVERSITY OF MANAGEMENT

Distance MBA Program
Fairfield, Iowa

Maharishi University of Management, founded in 1971, is an independent-nonprofit university. It is accredited by the North Central Association of Colleges and Schools. The Distance MBA Program first offered graduate business distance learning courses in 1995. In 1997–98, it offered 15 graduate business courses at a distance. In the fall of 1997, there were 350 students enrolled in distance learning graduate-level business courses and programs.

Course delivery sites Courses are delivered to 5 off-campus centers in Maharishi Nagar (India), Hyderabad (India), Lucknow (India), Bangalore (India), Madras (India).

Media Courses are delivered via videotapes, computer conferencing, print. Students and teachers may interact via telephone, e-mail, World Wide Web. The following equipment may be required: a TV and a VCR and/or a computer with access to the Internet.

Geographic service area/ restrictions Programs are available worldwide.

Services Distance learners have access to library services, e-mail services, academic advising, bookstore at a distance.

Credit-earning options Students may transfer credits from another institution or may earn credits through examinations, portfolio assessment.

Typical costs Tuition of $370 per unit. *Non-credit courses:* $370 per unit. Financial aid is available to distance learners.

Registration Students may register by mail.

Contact Ellen Smith, Director of Distance MBA Program, Maharishi University of Management, 1600 North Fourth Street, Fairfield, IA 52557. *Telephone:* 515-472-1216. *Fax:* 515-472-1191. *E-mail:* mba@mum. edu. *Web site:* http://www.mum.edu/ SBPA/distance.html.

DEGREE & CERTIFICATE PROGRAMS

Master of Business Administration (MBA)

In the fall of 1997 there were 350 students enrolled in this program. In 1996–97, 90 degrees were earned at a distance through this program.

Application requirements *Prior education:* Baccalaureate degree. *Other requirements:* GMAT, TOEFL (for international applicants), college transcripts, an essay or personal statement, letter(s) of recommendation, an application fee of $240.

Completion requirements 88 semester units. *Maximum time for completion:* seven years.

INDIVIDUAL COURSE SUBJECT AREAS

Graduate
Accounting; Banking; Finance; Human Resources; International Business; Management; Management Information Systems; Marketing

Noncredit
Accounting; Banking; Finance; Human Resources; International Business; Management; Management Information Systems; Marketing

MARYLHURST UNIVERSITY

Graduate Department of Management

Marylhurst, Oregon

Marylhurst University, founded in 1893, is an independent-religious Roman Catholic comprehensive institution. It is accredited by the Northwest Association of Schools and Colleges. The Graduate Department of Management first offered graduate business distance learning courses in 1997. In 1997–98, it offered 15 graduate business courses at a distance. In the fall of 1997, there were 35 students enrolled in distance learning graduate-level business courses and programs.

Course delivery sites Students can receive instruction anywhere.

Media Courses are delivered via World Wide Web. Students and teachers may meet in person or interact via mail, telephone, fax, e-mail, World Wide Web. The following equipment may be required: a computer (486 or better), Windows 95, a 14.4K modem, and access to the Internet.

Geographic service area/ restrictions Programs are available worldwide.

Services Distance learners have access to library services, academic advising, bookstore at a distance.

Typical costs Tuition of $250 per credit. Financial aid is available to distance learners.

Registration Students may register by mail, fax, phone, e-mail, World Wide Web.

Contact Kathleen Paul, Director, Marylhurst University, PO Box 261, 17600 Pacific Highway (Highway 43), Marylhurst, OR 97036. *Telephone:* 503-699-6246. *Fax:* 503-636-9526. *E-mail:* kpaul@marylhurst.edu.

DEGREE & CERTIFICATE PROGRAMS

Master of Business Administration (MBA)

Application requirements *Prior education:* Baccalaureate degree. *Other requirements:* GMAT, college transcripts, an essay or personal statement, letter(s) of recommendation, an application fee of $80, work experience, resume.

Completion requirements 60 quarter hours are required. *Maximum time for completion:* five years.

MARYLHURST UNIVERSITY

Graduate Department of Management

Marylhurst, Oregon

THE UNIVERSITY

Marylhurst University was founded in 1893 by the Sisters of the Holy Names as the first liberal arts college for women in the Pacific Northwest. In 1974, the University reorganized to become a coeducational institution and introduced a model of lifelong learning to the community. The institution serves a diverse student body of nearly 1,600 students. The University offers programs that lead to undergraduate degrees in art, communication, environmental science, fine arts, human studies, humanities, interdisciplinary studies, management, music, organizational communication, religious studies, science, and social sciences. Graduate degrees are offered in art therapy, business administration, and interdisciplinary studies. Fully accredited by the Northwest Association of Schools and Colleges, Marylhurst is a leader in competency-based education, Prior Learning Assessment, and delivering a liberal arts education across the Internet.

DISTANCE LEARNING PROGRAM

Continuing Marylhurst's legacy of serving previously underserved populations of learners, the distance learning program offers an opportunity to engage in a collaborative, highly interactive learning experience with flexibility and convenience. Undergraduate and graduate courses are offered; students may complete general education requirements and some majors through online courses.

The Master of Business Administration degree is a 45-credit graduate degree that focuses on key competencies and practical skills. Redesigned in 1998, the core curriculum is structured to meet the needs of highly motivated, working adults. It consists of 30 credits that develop expertise in core disciplines, with 9 to 12 credits in an area of specialization, including finance, marketing and sales, organizational effectiveness, or the new concentration in information and knowledge management, which is offered only on line. Opportunities for internships/practicums and portfolio development fulfill the remaining requirements. A newly developed ethics colloquium is offered on line as well as on-site.

DELIVERY MEDIA

Students need access to the Internet and a moderate level of comfort working on the World Wide Web to participate in online courses. Because courses are delivered via password-protected Web sites, students without personal computers may use public computing stations, such as those found in libraries. The Web-based delivery system incorporates private mail, conferencing, course materials, and other features. Specific courses may require specific software. Textbooks and other traditional study materials are routinely used with online courses.

SPECIAL PROGRAMS

The newest concentration in Marylhurst's M.B.A. program is an opportunity to study information and knowledge management. Available only on line, this concentration focuses on the ways that information and knowledge affect commerce and organizations. Students gain a greater understanding of the history of exchange, the psychological relationships that ground commerce, and the consequences that easy and inexpensive access to information has on doing business.

FACULTY

Marylhurst University faculty members are practitioner faculty members who apply their studies to the real world. Ninety-five percent of graduate faculty members hold doctoral degrees. The remainder hold master's degrees or terminal degrees in their fields.

STUDENT SERVICES

Students who take online courses have access to all materials and services available to students on campus. Remote access to library services, online registration, academic advising, financial aid information, and other services are available

through either the general Web site, password-protected sites, e-mail, or telephone.

CREDIT OPTIONS

Students may transfer up to 9 credits from other accredited institutions. The transfer of credits is subject to the approval of the Graduate Department of Management. On occasion, a student may be eligible to challenge select courses in the curriculum.

ADMISSION

Applicants must hold a bachelor's degree from an accredited institution (a business degree is not required), have substantial work experience, and complete the GMAT or GRE. Applications are accepted each quarter, and students may begin the program in any quarter.

TUITION AND FEES

Tuition for online courses is the same as the tuition for on-campus courses—$265 per credit hour. Supplemental fees include a technology fee of $4 per credit hour (up to 12 credits of enrollment) and a student services fee of $17 per term of enrollment.

FINANCIAL AID

All students at Marylhurst are eligible for the standard range of federal aid programs, including Federal Pell Grants and the Work-Study Program. Additional opportunities for aid come from state-sponsored programs and University and private scholarships. In 1997–98, $5.7 million was awarded to Marylhurst students from these combined sources, and 65 percent of Marylhurst students receive financial aid.

APPLYING

Students should apply to the M.B.A. program approximately six weeks prior to the beginning of the term. The submission of an application, a resume, a personal statement, three letters of recommendation, GMAT or GRE scores, and an $80 application fee is required for admission.

CONTACT

Dr. Bonita M. Kolb, Chair,
Graduate Studies in Business
Management

Dorothy Deline, Assistant to the
Chair and Program Advisor
Jennifer Ballard, Program Advisor
Graduate Department of
Management
Marylhurst University
17600 Pacific Highway (Highway
43)
P.O. Box 261
Marylhurst, Oregon 97036
Telephone: 503-699-6246
800-634-9982 (toll-free)
Fax: 503-636-9526
E-mail: mba@marylhurst.edu
Web site: http://www.marylhurst.
edu

MISSISSIPPI STATE UNIVERSITY

Office of Graduate Studies in Business
Mississippi State, Mississippi

Mississippi State University, founded in 1878, is a state-supported university. It is accredited by the Southern Association of Colleges and Schools. The Office of Graduate Studies in Business first offered graduate business distance learning courses in 1997. In 1997–98, it offered 10 graduate business courses at a distance. In the fall of 1997, there were 20 students enrolled in distance learning graduate-level business courses and programs.

Course delivery sites Courses are delivered to military bases, high schools, hospitals.

Media Courses are delivered via interactive television, World Wide Web, e-mail. Students and teachers may interact via mail, telephone, e-mail, interactive television, World Wide Web. The following equipment may be required: a computer with Windows 98.

Geographic service area/ restrictions Programs are available worldwide. Students must have completed the prerequisite courses before taking graduate-level courses.

Services Distance learners have access to library services, academic advising, bookstore at a distance.

Credit-earning options Students may transfer credits from another institu-

tion or may earn credits through military training.

Typical costs Tuition of $330 per course.

Registration Students may register by World Wide Web.

Contact Dr. Barbara A. Spencer, Director of Graduate Studies in Business, Mississippi State University, PO Drawer 5288, Mississippi State, MS 39762. *Telephone:* 601-325-1891. *Fax:* 601-325-8161. *E-mail:* bspencer@ cobilan.msstate.edu.

DEGREE & CERTIFICATE PROGRAMS

Master of Business Administration (MBA)

Application requirements *Prior education:* Baccalaureate degree. *Other requirements:* GMAT, college

transcripts, an essay or personal statement, letter(s) of recommendation, an application fee of $25.

Completion requirements 30 semester credit hours. *Maximum time for completion:* seven years.

MONASH UNIVERSITY
Clayton, Australia

Monash University is a university in Australia. It first offered graduate business distance learning courses in 1997. In 1997–98, it offered 2 graduate business courses at a distance. In the fall of 1997, there were 30 students enrolled in distance learning graduate-level business courses and programs.

Course delivery sites Students can receive instruction anywhere.

Media Courses are delivered via computer software, World Wide Web, e-mail, print. Students and teachers may meet in person or interact via mail, telephone, fax, e-mail, World Wide Web. The following equipment may be required: a computer with enough available memory to load Lotus Learning Space, access to the Internet, and a modem.

Geographic service area/restrictions Programs are available worldwide. Students must satisfy the entrance requirements for the MBA in order to enroll in distance learning courses.

Services Distance learners have access to library services, the campus computer network, e-mail services, bookstore at a distance.

Typical costs Tuition of $2000 per course. Tuition is in Australian dollars. *Non-credit courses:* $2000 Australian dollars per course.

Registration Students may register by mail, fax, e-mail, World Wide Web.

Contact Christine Montgomery, MBA Admissions Officer, Monash University, MBA Admissions, PO Box 2224, Caulfield Junction, Victoria, 3161, Australia. *Telephone:* 61-392151850. *Fax:* 61-392151821. *E-mail:* genmba@mteliza.edu.au.

INDIVIDUAL COURSE SUBJECT AREAS

Graduate
Business Ethics; International Business

Noncredit
Business Ethics; International Business

NATIONAL–LOUIS UNIVERSITY

College of Business and Management
Evanston, Illinois

National–Louis University, founded in 1886, is an independent-nonprofit university. It is accredited by the North Central Association of Colleges and Schools. The College of Business and Management first offered graduate business distance learning courses in 1997. In 1997–98, it offered 2 graduate business courses at a distance.

Course delivery sites Students can receive instruction anywhere.

Media Courses are delivered via World Wide Web. Students and teachers may meet in person or interact via mail, telephone, fax, e-mail, World Wide Web. The following equipment may be required: a computer with access to the Internet and email.

Geographic service area/restrictions Programs are available worldwide.

Services Distance learners have access to library services, e-mail services at a distance.

Typical costs Tuition of $199 per semester hour. *Non-credit courses:* $81.00 per day. Costs may vary by number of credits taken, course delivery options. Financial aid is available to distance learners.

Registration Students may register by mail, fax, phone, e-mail, World Wide Web.

Contact Dr. Angela Durante, Director of Continuing Education, National–Louis University, Office of Continuing Education, 1000 Capitol Drive, Wheeling, IL 60090. *Telephone:* 800-443-5522, Ext. 5495. *Fax:* 847-465-0593. *E-mail:* gext@wheeling1.nl.edu. *Web site:* http://www.nluconted.edu.

INDIVIDUAL COURSE SUBJECT AREAS

Graduate
Management Information Systems

Noncredit
Management Information Systems

NAVAL POSTGRADUATE SCHOOL

Systems Management Department
Monterey, California

Naval Postgraduate School is a federally supported graduate institution. It is accredited by the Western Association of Schools and Colleges, Inc. The Systems Management Department first offered graduate business distance learning courses in 1995. In 1997–98, it offered 40 graduate business courses at a distance. In the fall of 1997, there were 90 students enrolled in distance learning graduate-level business courses and programs.

Course delivery sites Courses are delivered to your workplace, military bases.

Media Courses are delivered via videoconferencing, print. Students and teachers may meet in person or interact via videoconferencing, telephone, e-mail, World Wide Web.

Geographic service area/restrictions Programs are available nationwide. Students must be employees of either the Department of Defense or the Department of the Navy.

Services Distance learners have access to library services at a distance.

Registration Students may register by mail.

Contact Gail Fann Thomas, Associate Chair for Instruction, Naval Postgraduate School, 555 Dyer Road, Building 330, CODE SM/Fa, Monterey, CA 93943. *Telephone:* 831-656-2756. *Fax:* 831-656-3407. *E-mail:* gthomas@nps.navy.mil.

DEGREE & CERTIFICATE PROGRAMS

Master of Science (MS)

Geographic service area/restrictions Students must be employees of either the Department of Defense or the Department of the Navy.

Application requirements *Prior education:* Baccalaureate degree. *Other requirements:* college transcripts, an essay or personal statement, letter(s) of recommendation, work experience.

Completion requirements 48 quarter hours are required.

On-campus requirements The program requires eight weeks of residency on campus.

INDIVIDUAL COURSE SUBJECT AREAS

Graduate
Contract Management

NEW YORK INSTITUTE OF TECHNOLOGY

School of Management
Old Westbury, New York

New York Institute of Technology, founded in 1955, is an independent-nonprofit comprehensive institution. It is accredited by the Middle States Association of Colleges and Schools. The School of Management first offered graduate business distance learning courses in 1998.

Course delivery sites Students can receive instruction anywhere.

Media Courses are delivered via World Wide Web. Students and teachers may meet in person or interact via mail, telephone, fax, e-mail, World Wide Web. The following equipment may be required: a computer with a web browser and access to the Internet.

Geographic service area/restrictions Programs are available worldwide.

Services Distance learners have access to library services, e-mail services, academic advising at a distance.

Credit-earning options Students may transfer credits from another institution or may earn credits through examinations, portfolio assessment, military training, business training.

Typical costs Tuition of $413 per credit. Financial aid is available to distance learners.

Registration Students may register by mail, fax, phone, e-mail, World Wide Web.

Contact Glenn Berman, Executive Director of Admissions, New York Institute of Technology, PO Box 8000, Old Westbury, NY 11568. *Telephone:* 800-345-NYIT. *Fax:* 516-686-7613. *E-mail:* gberman@iris.nyit.edu. *Web site:* http://www.nyit.edu.

DEGREE & CERTIFICATE PROGRAMS

Master of Business Administration (MBA)

Application requirements *Prior education:* Baccalaureate degree. *Other requirements:* GMAT, GRE, college transcripts, an essay or personal statement, an application fee of $50.

Completion requirements 36–42 credits.

On-campus requirements One program option requires an on-campus oral exam.

INDIVIDUAL COURSE SUBJECT AREAS

Graduate
Accounting; Finance; International Business; Management Information Systems; Marketing

NORTH DAKOTA STATE UNIVERSITY

College of Business Administration
Fargo, North Dakota

North Dakota State University, founded in 1890, is a state-supported university. It is accredited by the North Central Association of Colleges and Schools. In 1997–98, it offered 3 graduate business courses at a distance. In the fall of 1997, there were 8 students enrolled in distance learning graduate-level business courses and programs.

Course delivery sites Courses are delivered to your workplace, Minot State University (Minot), North Dakota State College of Science (Wahpeton), Valley City State University (Valley City).

Media Courses are delivered via interactive television. Students and teachers may meet in person or interact via mail, telephone, e-mail, interactive television.

Geographic service area/restrictions Programs are available statewide.

Services Distance learners have access to academic advising, career placement assistance at a distance.

Credit-earning options Students may transfer credits from another institution or may earn credits through examinations.

Typical costs Tuition of $1286 per semester plus mandatory fees of $230 per semester for in-state residents. Tuition of $3434 per semester plus mandatory fees of $230 per semester for out-of-state residents. *Non-credit courses:* 50% of the regular tuition charge. Costs may vary by number of credits taken. Financial aid is available to distance learners.

Registration Students may register by phone.

Contact Paul Brown, Assistant MBA Director, North Dakota State University, PO Box 5137, Putnam Hall, Fargo, ND 58105. *Telephone:* 701-231-7681. *Fax:* 701-231-7508. *E-mail:* pabrown@plains.nodak.edu. *Web site:* http://www.ndsu.nodak.edu/cba/.

DEGREE & CERTIFICATE PROGRAMS

Master of Business Administration (MBA)

In the fall of 1997 there were 8 students enrolled in this program. In 1996–97, 2 degrees were earned at a distance through this program.

Application requirements *Prior education:* Baccalaureate degree in business. *Other requirements:* GRE, college transcripts, letter(s) of recommendation, an application fee of $25.

Completion requirements 30 semester credits are required. *Maximum time for completion:* seven years.

On-campus requirements Students must take an Exit exam on campus.

INDIVIDUAL COURSE SUBJECT AREAS

Graduate
Finance; Human Resources; Managerial Economics; Operations Management

GRADUATE SCHOOL OF BUSINESS ZURICH

Zurich, Switzerland

Graduate School of Business Zurich is an institution of higher education in Switzerland. It first offered graduate business distance learning courses in 1991. In 1997–98, it offered 25 graduate business courses at a distance. In the fall of 1997, there were 1,250 students enrolled in distance learning graduate-level business courses and programs.

Course delivery sites Students can receive instruction anywhere.

Media Courses are delivered via videotapes, videoconferencing, audiotapes, computer software, CD-ROM, computer conferencing, World Wide Web, e-mail, print. Students and teachers may meet in person or interact via videoconferencing, mail, telephone, fax, e-mail, World Wide Web. The following equipment may be required: a laptop computer with access to the Internet and email.

Geographic service area/restrictions Programs are available throughout Europe. Students must be at least 30 years old, have an academic degree, and have five years of experience in leadership.

Services Distance learners have access to library services, the campus computer network, e-mail services, academic advising, tutoring, bookstore at a distance.

Credit-earning options Students may earn credits through examinations, portfolio assessment.

Typical costs Contact school for information.

Registration Students may register by mail, fax, phone, e-mail, World Wide Web.

Contact Mr. Heinrich Brügger, Admissions Officer, Graduate School of Business Zurich, GSPA Zürich, Schühoengasse 4, Zurich, CH-8001, Switzerland. *Telephone:* 004-112116047. *Fax:* 004-112110984. *E-mail:* info@gsba.ch. *Web site:* http://www.gsba.ch.

DEGREE & CERTIFICATE PROGRAMS

Master of Business Administration (MBA)

Geographic service area/restrictions Program is available throughout Europe.

Application requirements *Prior education:* Baccalaureate degree. *Minimum age:* 30. *Other requirements:* GMAT, TOEFL (for international applicants), college transcripts, an essay or personal statement, letter(s) of recommendation, an application fee of 150 Swiss Francs, work experience, interview, five years of experience in leadership.

Completion requirements 10 courses are required. *Maximum time for completion:* four years.

On-campus requirements Students must be on campus six times for two weeks.

Master of Science in Finance (MS)

Geographic service area/ restrictions Program is available throughout Europe.

Application requirements *Prior education:* Baccalaureate degree. *Minimum age:* 30. *Other requirements:* GMAT, TOEFL (for international applicants), college transcripts, an essay or personal statement, letter(s) of recommendation, an application fee of 150 Swiss Francs, work experience, interview, five years of experience in leadership.

Completion requirements 10 courses are required. *Maximum time for completion:* four years.

On-campus requirements Students must be on campus six times for two weeks.

Master of Science in Logistics (MS)

Geographic service area/ restrictions Program is available throughout Europe.

Application requirements *Prior education:* Baccalaureate degree. *Minimum age:* 30. *Other requirements:* GMAT, TOEFL (for international applicants), college transcripts, an essay or personal statement, letter(s) of recommendation, an application fee of 150 Swiss Francs, work experience, interview, five years of experience in leadership.

Completion requirements 10 courses are required. *Maximum time for completion:* four years.

On-campus requirements Students must be on campus six times for two weeks.

Master of Science in MIS/IT (MS)

Geographic service area/ restrictions Program is available throughout Europe.

Application requirements *Prior education:* Baccalaureate degree. *Minimum age:* 30. *Other requirements:* GMAT, TOEFL (for international applicants), college transcripts, an essay or personal statement, letter(s) of recommendation, an application fee of 150 Swiss Francs, work experience, interview, five years of experience in leadership.

Completion requirements 10 courses are required. *Maximum time for completion:* four years.

On-campus requirements Students must be on campus six times for two weeks.

OHIO UNIVERSITY
College of Business
Athens, Ohio

Ohio University, founded in 1804, is a state-supported university. It is accredited by the North Central Association of Colleges and Schools. The College of Business first offered graduate business distance learning courses in 1997. In the fall of 1997, there were 22 students enrolled in distance learning graduate-level business courses and programs.

Course delivery sites Students can receive instruction anywhere.

Media Courses are delivered via videotapes, computer conferencing, World Wide Web, e-mail. Students and teachers may meet in person or interact via mail, telephone, fax, e-mail, World Wide Web. The following equipment may be required: a computer with access to the Internet. All necessary software is provided in the tuition package.

Geographic service area/restrictions Programs are available nationwide.

Services Distance learners have access to library services, the campus computer network, e-mail services, career placement assistance at a distance.

Typical costs Tuition of $29,000 per degree program.

Contact Richard G. Milter, Director, MBA Without Boundaries, Ohio University, Copeland Hall, Athens, OH 45701. *Telephone:* 800-622-3124. *Fax:* 740-593-1388. *E-mail:* milter@ohiou.edu. *Web site:* http://oumba.cob.ohiou.edu/~oumba/.

DEGREE & CERTIFICATE PROGRAMS

Master of Business Administration (MBA)

In the fall of 1997 there were 22 students enrolled in this program.

Application requirements *Prior education:* Baccalaureate degree. *Other requirements:* college transcripts, an essay or personal statement, letter(s) of recommendation, work experience, interview.

Completion requirements 72 quarter hours are required. *Maximum time for completion:* two years.

On-campus requirements Students must complete nine residencies within two years.

OHIO UNIVERSITY

College of Business
MBA Without Boundaries

Athens, Ohio

THE UNIVERSITY

Ohio University, founded in 1804, was the first institution of higher learning in the Northwest Territory. The total enrollment of the Athens campus is approximately 19,000, while the regional campuses enroll more than 7,900 additional students. The present graduate enrollment is about 2,900. The full-time faculty numbers 865.

Ohio University offers master's degrees in nearly all its major academic divisions and doctoral degrees in selected departments. The University is accredited by the North Central Association of Colleges and Schools and by the recognized professional accrediting associations that are identified with its major academic divisions, such as AACSB–The International Association for Management Education for the College of Business.

Ohio University has also been a leader in providing learning opportunities for nontraditional students, including correspondence study, credit for college-level learning, external degree programs, and electronic course delivery.

DISTANCE LEARNING PROGRAM

The Ohio University MBA Without Boundaries offers an innovative approach to executive education. The program is based on a proven structure of project-based instruction and action-learning methodology. The convenience of online, interactive learning is combined with intense, high-quality residencies that offer personal interaction and collegial collaboration. The result is an M.B.A. program with an innovative learning architecture that is specifically designed to provide working professionals with the skills they need to succeed in the twenty-first century.

Pioneered by Ohio University business faculty members more than a decade ago, this approach to M.B.A. education is continually perfected. Innovative technology and online collaborative learning enhance business education and leadership development. Using a holistic approach to business education that eliminates boundaries between disciplines, participants are challenged by experiences similar to those that will be faced by leaders in tomorrow's business world during the M.B.A. program

DELIVERY MEDIA

The virtual community that permeates and enables the MBA Without Boundaries is built upon electronic collaboration among participants and faculty members, electronic access to learning materials, and electronic tutoring by the faculty and outside experts. Program participants utilize the MBA Without Boundaries Intranet to access learning modules and perform individual research, collaborate with other members of their learning teams, and interact with the faculty.

The MBA Without Boundaries Intranet serves as an interactive resource center that includes materials prepared and posted by faculty members and a collaboration center, where members of learning teams ask questions and post responses. A tutorial center is provided, where participants can respond to the questions of faculty members and other participants and meet with other participants synchronously. Live audio and video conferences that use microwave and compressed video signals allow participants to communicate with experts from around the world. Multimedia learning materials, online video and audio inputs, and CD-ROM textbooks provide additional sources for information access.

SPECIAL PROGRAMS

The program is built around nine major learning projects and requires a two-year commitment. Each project begins and ends during a residency. There are three 1-week residencies, one each at the beginning, middle, and end of the program. Three weekend residencies are also held each year. Residencies are intense, face-to-face learning experiences with other participants and faculty members. During residencies, the concentration is aimed at the start-up of projects, project deliverables, and learning outcomes. Participants are also provided with content modules on relevant topics and interact in workshops that focus on the development of leadership

skills. An optional two-week international consulting project is also available to program participants.

FACULTY

The MBA Without Boundaries faculty team consists of core College of Business faculty members, with additional expertise from academic institutions and industry available as needed. The faculty members on the team have extensive business backgrounds and represent various industries. They also have solid teaching and research experience, including contemporary research that targets learning platforms that incorporate electronic collaboration and other innovative learning approaches.

CREDIT OPTIONS

This program is project-based and lockstepped. Participants must enroll in the MBA Without Boundaries program for the full two years. A total of 72 graduate credit hours is earned. No transfer of credits is permitted.

ADMISSION

The MBA Without Boundaries is designed for individuals who are already well on the road to success, have demonstrated their drive and capability through at least two to four years of increasing responsibility, and want to be leaders of information-age organizations in the next century.

In making the selection decision, past accomplishments (as demonstrated through work experience), letters of nomination and recommendation, responses to questions on the M.B.A. admission questionnaire, and prior academic performance are considered. A personal interview is required of each finalist.

To be considered for admission, students must submit two sets of official transcripts from all undergraduate and graduate programs attended, arrange for a letter of nomination to be sent from a representative of their company along with two other letters of recommendation, and complete the M.B.A. admission questionnaire.

TUITION AND FEES

Total tuition and fees for the entire MBA Without Boundaries program are $30,000. These costs include tuition, private hotel room and breakfast for all residencies, special group dinners during residencies, a notebook computer with all relevant software, a reference library, and other materials used during the program. Participants are responsible for personal travel to and from the residencies and for access to an Internet service provider. Tuition is payable prior to each of the nine residencies. There are no additional fees for non-Ohio residents.

FINANCIAL AID

Financial aid may be available. For further information, students should visit the Web site at http://www-sfa. chubb.ohiou.edu.

APPLYING

All application materials can be found on line at the address listed below. These materials can be requested by mail as well.

CONTACT

Richard G. Milter, Ph.D.
Program Director
MBA Without Boundaries
College of Business
310 Copeland Hall
Ohio University
Athens, Ohio 45701-2979
Telephone: 740-593-2072
         800-622-3124 (toll-free)
E-mail: milter@ohiou.edu
Web site: http://mbawb.cob.ohiou.
   edu

OKLAHOMA STATE UNIVERSITY

College of Business Administration
Stillwater, Oklahoma

Oklahoma State University, founded in 1890, is a state-supported university. It is accredited by the North Central Association of Colleges and Schools. The College of Business Administration first offered graduate business distance learning courses in 1991. In 1997–98, it offered 16 graduate business courses at a distance. In the fall of 1997, there were 100 students enrolled in distance learning graduate-level business courses and programs.

Course delivery sites Courses are delivered to your workplace, 3 off-campus centers in Oklahoma City, Ponca City, Tulsa.

Media Courses are delivered via videotapes, interactive television, World Wide Web, e-mail. Students and teachers may interact via mail, telephone, e-mail, interactive television, World Wide Web. The following equipment may be required: access to a studio to receive the television signal.

Geographic service area/ restrictions Programs are available in Oklahoma and neighboring states. Students must meet the program entrance requirements.

Services Distance learners have access to library services, the campus computer network, e-mail services, academic advising, bookstore at a distance.

Credit-earning options Students may earn credits through examinations.

Typical costs Tuition of $195 per credit.

Registration Students may register by mail, phone.

Contact Ms. Alexa Bargmann, Distance Learning Coordinator, Oklahoma State University, 215 College of Business Administration, Stillwater, OK 74078. *Telephone:* 405-744-5208.

DEGREE & CERTIFICATE PROGRAMS

Master of Business Administration (MBA)

Geographic service area/ restrictions Program is available in Oklahoma and neighboring states.

Application requirements *Prior education:* Baccalaureate degree. *Other requirements:* GMAT, GRE, college transcripts, an essay or personal statement, letter(s) of recommendation, an application fee of $25, work experience.

Completion requirements 50 hours are required. *Maximum time for completion:* five years.

Master of Science (MS)

Geographic service area/ restrictions Program is available in Oklahoma and neighboring states.

Application requirements *Prior education:* Baccalaureate degree. *Other requirements:* GMAT, GRE, college transcripts, an essay or personal statement, letter(s) of recommendation, an application fee of $25, work experience.

Completion requirements 33 hours are required. *Maximum time for completion:* five years.

OLD DOMINION UNIVERSITY

MBA Program
Norfolk, Virginia

Old Dominion University, founded in 1930, is a state-supported university. It is accredited by the Southern Association of Colleges and Schools. The MBA Program first offered graduate business distance learning courses in 1997. In 1997–98, it offered 22 graduate business courses at a distance. In the fall of 1997, there were 24 students enrolled in distance learning graduate-level business courses and programs.

Course delivery sites Courses are delivered to your workplace, military bases, other colleges, off-campus center(s).

Media Courses are delivered via televison. Students and teachers may meet in person or interact via videoconferencing, mail, telephone, fax, e-mail, interactive television, World Wide Web. The following equipment may be required: a computer.

Geographic service area/restrictions Programs are available worldwide. Students must meet the admissions standards for the MBA program.

Services Distance learners have access to library services, the campus computer network, e-mail services, academic advising, bookstore at a distance.

Credit-earning options Students may transfer credits from another institution or may earn credits through examinations, portfolio assessment.

Typical costs Tuition of $180 per credit for in-state residents. Tuition of $359 per credit for out-of-state residents. Costs may vary by campus or location. Financial aid is available to distance learners.

Registration Students may register by mail, fax, phone, e-mail.

Contact Jeanie Kline, Director, TELETECHNET, Old Dominion University, Norfolk, VA 23529. *Telephone:* 757-683-3163. *E-mail:* jkline@odu.edu.

DEGREE & CERTIFICATE PROGRAMS

Master of Business Administration (MBA)

In the fall of 1997 there were 24 students enrolled in this program.

Application requirements *Prior education:* Baccalaureate degree. *Other requirements:* GMAT, college transcripts, an essay or personal statement, letter(s) of recommendation, an application fee of $30.

Completion requirements 49 credit hours are required. *Maximum time for completion:* six years.

INDIVIDUAL COURSE SUBJECT AREAS

Graduate
Accounting; City/Urban Administration; Economics; Finance; Information Management; Management; Marketing; Operations Management; Taxation

OPEN UNIVERSITY OF THE NETHERLANDS

Department of Economics, Public and Business Administration

Heerlen, Netherlands

Open University of the Netherlands is a university in the Netherlands. The Department of Economics, Public and Business Administration first offered graduate business distance learning courses in 1984.

Course delivery sites Courses are delivered to your home, your workplace, 6 off-campus centers in Jyvarhyle (Finland), Dublin (Ireland), Oldenburg (Germany), Aix-en-Provence (France), Nantes (France).

Media Courses are delivered via videotapes, audioconferencing, computer software, CD-ROM, World Wide Web, e-mail, print. Students and teachers may meet in person or interact via telephone, e-mail, Lotus Notes. The following equipment may be required: a computer (486 or better) with a modem and access to the Internet.

Geographic service area/ restrictions Programs are available worldwide. Students need a bachelor's degree, three years work experience and fluency in the English language.

Services Distance learners have access to library services, the campus computer network, e-mail services, academic advising, tutoring at a distance.

Credit-earning options Students may earn credits through examinations.

Typical costs Students pay 300 FL per module (3 credits).

Registration Students may register by mail, fax.

Contact Dr. Ron Tuninga, Director of EuroMBA, Open University of the Netherlands, Valkenburgerweg 167, Heerlen, 6419 AT, Netherlands. *Telephone:* 045-5762404. *Fax:* 045-5762103. *E-mail:* ron.tuninga@ouh.nl.

DEGREE & CERTIFICATE PROGRAMS

Master of Business Administration (MBA)

In the fall of 1997 there were 30 students enrolled in this program.

Application requirements *Prior education:* Baccalaureate degree. *Other requirements:* college transcripts, an essay or personal statement, letter(s) of recommendation, an application fee, work experience, fluency in the English language.

Completion requirements 1800 hours are required. *Maximum time for completion:* three years.

INDIVIDUAL COURSE SUBJECT AREAS

Graduate
Accounting; Business Policy/Strategy; Commerce; Economics; European Business Studies; Financial Management/Planning; International Business; International Marketing

PENNSYLVANIA STATE UNIVERSITY AT ERIE, THE BEHREND COLLEGE

Continuing and Distance Education Office

Erie, Pennsylvania

Pennsylvania State University at Erie, The Behrend College, founded in 1948, is a state-related comprehensive institution. It is accredited by the Middle States Association of Colleges and Schools. The Continuing and Distance Education Office first offered graduate business distance learning courses in 1995. In 1997–98, it offered 5 graduate business courses at a distance.

Course delivery sites Courses are delivered to Jamestown Community College (Jamestown, NY).

Media Courses are delivered via televison, videoconferencing. Students and teachers may interact via videoconferencing.

Geographic service area/restrictions Programs are available locally. Students must be admitted to the Penn State Erie MBA program.

Services Distance learners have access to library services, the campus computer network, e-mail services, academic advising at a distance.

Credit-earning options Students may transfer credits from another institution.

Typical costs Tuition of $305 per credit for in-state residents. Tuition of $409 per credit for out-of-state residents. Costs may vary by campus or location, number of credits taken. Financial aid is available to distance learners.

Registration Students may register by phone.

Contact Jane Brady, Assistant Director of Admissions and Financial Aid, Pennsylvania State University at Erie, The Behrend College, 5091 Station Road, Erie, PA 16563. *Telephone:* 814-898-6100. *Fax:* 814-898-6044. *E-mail:* jub9@psu.edu. *Web site:* http://www.pserie.psu.edu.

DEGREE & CERTIFICATE PROGRAMS

Master of Business Administration (MBA)

Application requirements *Prior education:* Baccalaureate degree. *Other requirements:* GMAT, college transcripts, an essay or personal statement, letter(s) of recommendation, an application fee of $40.

Completion requirements 48 credits are required. *Other requirements:* courses offered via distance education are contingent upon sufficient enrollment and may make it necessary to take a class on-campus if enrollment is too low to offer through distance learning. *Maximum time for completion:* eight years.

PURDUE UNIVERSITY

Krannert Executive Education Programs
West Lafayette, Indiana

Purdue University, founded in 1869, is a state-supported university. It is accredited by the North Central Association of Colleges and Schools. The Krannert Executive Education Program first offered graduate business distance learning courses in 1983. In 1997–98, it offered 260 graduate business courses at a distance. In the fall of 1997, there were 230 students enrolled in distance learning graduate-level business courses and programs.

Course delivery sites Courses are delivered to your home, your workplace, Budapest University of Economic Sciences (Budapest, Hungary), Tilburg University (Tilburg, Netherlands).

Media Courses are delivered via computer software, computer conferencing, World Wide Web, e-mail. Students and teachers may meet in person or interact via mail, e-mail, World Wide Web. The following equipment may be required: a computer with access to the Internet.

Geographic service area/ restrictions Programs are available worldwide.

Services Distance learners have access to academic advising, tutoring at a distance.

Typical costs Tuition of $12,500 per semester. Financial aid is available to distance learners.

Contact Dr. Martin Rapisarda, Director, Purdue University, 1310 Krannert Center, Suite 206, West Lafayette, IN 47907. *Telephone:* 765-494-7700. *Fax:* 765-494-0862. *E-mail:* rapisarda@mgmt.purdue.edu. *Web site:* http://www2.mgmt.purdue.edu/execed.

DEGREE & CERTIFICATE PROGRAMS

Master of Science in Management (MSM)

In the fall of 1997 there were 230 students enrolled in this program. In 1996–97, 115 degrees were earned at a distance through this program.

Application requirements *Prior education:* Baccalaureate degree. *Other requirements:* GMAT, college transcripts, an essay or personal statement, letter(s) of recommendation, an application fee of $30, work experience.

Completion requirements 48 credit hours are required. *Maximum time for completion:* 22 months.

On-campus requirements Students must attend six two-week residencies within the 22 month program.

REGENT UNIVERSITY
School of Business
Virginia Beach, Virginia

Regent University is an independent-nonprofit graduate institution. It is accredited by the Southern Association of Colleges and Schools. The School of Business first offered graduate business distance learning courses in 1990. In 1997–98, it offered 35 graduate business courses at a distance. In the fall of 1997, there were 125 students enrolled in distance learning graduate-level business courses and programs.

Course delivery sites Students can receive instruction anywhere.

Media Courses are delivered via videotapes, audiotapes, World Wide Web, e-mail, print. Students and teachers may meet in person or interact via audioconferencing, mail, telephone, e-mail. The following equipment may be required: a computer (Pentium preferred) with MS Office and access to the Internet.

Geographic service area/restrictions Programs are available worldwide. Students must be admitted into the degree program.

Services Distance learners have access to library services, academic advising, career placement assistance at a distance.

Credit-earning options Students may transfer credits from another institution or may earn credits through examinations.

Typical costs Tuition of $325 per unit plus mandatory fees of $6 per course. *Non-credit courses:* audit courses are half of regular tuition. Financial aid is available to distance learners.

Registration Students may register by World Wide Web.

Contact Tom Stansbury, Director of Marketing, Recruitment, and Admissions, Regent University, Regent University School of Business, 1000 Regent University Drive, Virginia Beach, VA 23464. *Telephone:* 800-477-3642. *Fax:* 757-226-4369. *E-mail:* busschool@regent.edu. *Web site:* http://regent.edu.

DEGREE & CERTIFICATE PROGRAMS

Master of Arts (MA)

Application requirements *Prior education:* Baccalaureate degree. *Other requirements:* college transcripts, letter(s) of recommendation, an application fee of $40, application form (no charge), resume.

Completion requirements 39 credits are required. *Maximum time for completion:* five years.

On-campus requirements Students must complete two five-day residencies on campus.

Master of Business Administration (MBA)

Application requirements *Prior education:* Baccalaureate degree. *Other requirements:* college transcripts, letter(s) of recommendation, an application fee of $40, application form (no charge), resume.

Completion requirements 57 credits are required. *Maximum time for completion:* five years.

On-campus requirements Students must complete two five-day residencies on campus.

INDIVIDUAL COURSE SUBJECT AREAS

Graduate

Accounting; Entrepreneurship; Finance; Management; Marketing; Nonprofit Management

REGIS UNIVERSITY

Denver, Colorado

Regis University, founded in 1877, is an independent-religious Roman Catholic (Jesuit) comprehensive institution. It is accredited by the North Central Association of Colleges and Schools. It first offered graduate business distance learning courses in 1997. In 1997–98, it offered 13 graduate business courses at a distance. In the fall of 1997, there were 200 students enrolled in distance learning graduate-level business courses and programs.

Course delivery sites Students can receive instruction anywhere.

Media Courses are delivered via videotapes, audiotapes, World Wide Web, e-mail, print. Students and teachers may interact via telephone, fax, e-mail, World Wide Web. The following equipment may be required: a computer (486 or better) with access to the Internet and email. Spreadsheet and word processing software is recommended. Courses may also require a TV and a VCR.

Geographic service area/ restrictions Programs are available worldwide. Applicants must meet admission standards for Regis University Graduate Programs.

Services Distance learners have access to library services, academic advising, career placement assistance, bookstore at a distance.

Credit-earning options Students may transfer credits from another institution.

Typical costs Tuition of $1035 per course. Students pay a one-time $80 graduation fee. Financial aid is available to distance learners.

Registration Students may register by mail, fax, phone, e-mail, World Wide Web.

Contact EMBA Information, Regis University, 9417 Princess Palm Avenue, Suite 175, Tampa, FL 33619-8317. *Telephone:* 888-MBA-REGIS. *Fax:* 813-628-6124. *E-mail:* enroll@ mbaregis.com. *Web site:* http://www. mbaregis.com.

DEGREE & CERTIFICATE PROGRAMS

Master of Business Administration (MBA)

In the fall of 1997 there were 200 students enrolled in this program.

Application requirements *Prior education:* Baccalaureate degree. *Other requirements:* college transcripts, an essay or personal statement, letter(s) of recommendation, an application fee of $75, work experience, resume.

Completion requirements 30 credit hours are required. *Maximum time for completion:* six years.

RENSSELAER POLYTECHNIC INSTITUTE

Lally School of Management and Technology
Troy, New York

Rensselaer Polytechnic Institute, founded in 1824, is an independent-nonprofit university. It is accredited by the Middle States Association of Colleges and Schools. The Lally School of Management and Technology first offered graduate business distance learning courses in 1995. In 1997–98, it offered 15 graduate business courses at a distance. In the fall of 1997, there were 100 students enrolled in distance learning graduate-level business courses and programs.

Course delivery sites Courses are delivered to your workplace.

Media Courses are delivered via television, videotapes, videoconferencing, World Wide Web. Students and teachers may meet in person or interact via videoconferencing, mail, telephone, fax, e-mail, World Wide Web.

Geographic service area/ restrictions Programs are available worldwide. Students must be employees of corporate partners.

Services Distance learners have access to the campus computer network, e-mail services, academic advising at a distance.

Credit-earning options Students may transfer credits from another institution.

Typical costs Tuition of $600 per credit. *Non-credit courses:* varies.

Registration Students may register by mail, fax, World Wide Web.

Contact Christine Katchmar, Director, Continuing and Distance Education, Rensselaer Polytechnic Institute, C11 4011, Troy, NY 12180. *Telephone:* 518-276-7787. *Fax:* 518-276-8026. *E-mail:* katchc@rpi.edu. *Web site:* http://lallyschool.rpi.edu.

DEGREE & CERTIFICATE PROGRAMS

Master of Business Administration (MBA)

Geographic service area/ restrictions Students must be the employees of corporate partners.

Application requirements *Prior education:* Baccalaureate degree. *Other requirements:* GMAT, college transcripts, an essay or personal statement, letter(s) of recommendation, an application fee of $35, work experience, supervisor's approval.

Completion requirements 60 credit hours are required. *Maximum time for completion:* five years.

Master of Science (MS)

Geographic service area/ restrictions Students must be the employees of corporate partners.

Application requirements *Prior education:* Baccalaureate degree. *Other requirements:* GMAT, college transcripts, an essay or personal statement, letter(s) of recommendation, an application fee of $35, work experience, supervisor's approval.

Completion requirements 30 credit hours are required. *Maximum time for completion:* five years.

INDIVIDUAL COURSE SUBJECT AREAS

Graduate
Accounting; Business Ethics; Economics; Finance; Management; Managerial Economics; Manufacturing Management; Technology Management

SALVE REGINA UNIVERSITY

Graduate Extension Study
Newport, Rhode Island

Salve Regina University, founded in 1934, is an independent-religious Roman Catholic comprehensive institution. It is accredited by the New England Association of Schools and Colleges. The Graduate Extension Study first offered graduate business distance learning courses in 1985. In 1997–98, it offered 15 graduate business courses at a distance. In the fall of 1997, there were 90 students enrolled in distance learning graduate-level business courses and programs.

Course delivery sites Students can receive instruction anywhere.

Media Courses are delivered via World Wide Web, e-mail, print. Students and teachers may meet in person or interact via mail, telephone, fax, e-mail, World Wide Web.

Geographic service area/ restrictions Programs are available worldwide. Students must have a bachelor's degree.

Services Distance learners have access to library services, the campus computer network, e-mail services, academic advising at a distance.

Credit-earning options Students may transfer credits from another institution or may earn credits through military training, business training.

Typical costs Tuition of $275 per credit plus mandatory fees of $75 per course. Financial aid is available to distance learners.

Registration Students may register by mail, fax, phone, e-mail, World Wide Web.

Contact Leona Misto, RSM, Director, Graduate Extension Studies, Salve Regina University, 100 Ochre Point Avenue, Newport, RI 02840-4192. *Telephone:* 800-637-0002. *Fax:* 401-849-0702. *E-mail:* mistol@salve. edu. *Web site:* http://www.salve.edu.

DEGREE & CERTIFICATE PROGRAMS

Master of Arts (MA)

Application requirements *Prior education:* Baccalaureate degree. *Other*

requirements: GMAT, MAT, or GRE, college transcripts, an essay or personal statement, letter(s) of recommendation, an application fee of $35.

Completion requirements 36 semester hours are required. *Maximum time for completion:* five years.

On-campus requirements Students must complete an on-campus residency or attend the Graduate Extension Study Institute.

Master of Science (MS)

Application requirements *Prior education:* Baccalaureate degree. *Other requirements:* GMAT, MAT, or GRE, college transcripts, an essay or personal

statement, letter(s) of recommendation, an application fee of $35.

Completion requirements 36 semester hours are required. *Maximum time for completion:* five years.

On-campus requirements Students must complete an on-campus residency or attend the Graduate Extension Study Institute.

INDIVIDUAL COURSE SUBJECT AREAS

Graduate
Management; Management Information Systems

SAN JOSE STATE UNIVERSITY

College of Business
San Jose, California

San Jose State University, founded in 1857, is a state-supported comprehensive institution. It is accredited by the Western Association of Schools and Colleges, Inc. The College of Business first offered graduate business distance learning courses in 1996. In 1997–98, it offered 4 graduate business courses at a distance. In the fall of 1997, there were 12 students enrolled in distance learning graduate-level business courses and programs.

Course delivery sites Courses are delivered to your workplace.

Media Courses are delivered via televison, videoconferencing, interactive television, e-mail. Students and teachers may interact via videoconferencing, telephone, fax, e-mail, interactive television, World Wide Web.

Geographic service area/restrictions Programs are available statewide. Students must be matriculated at San Jose State University and meet the program requirements.

Services Distance learners have access to bookstore at a distance.

Credit-earning options Students may transfer credits from another institution.

Typical costs Students pay $675 for up to 5.9 units and $1,008.50 for 6 or more units. Nonresident students pay an additional $246 per unit in fees. *Non-credit courses:* $465 per course. Costs may vary by number of credits taken.

Registration Students may register by mail, fax, phone, e-mail.

Contact Business Graduate Programs, San Jose State University, One Washington Square—BT250, San Jose, CA 95192-0162. *Telephone:* 408-924-3420. *Fax:* 408-924-3426. *E-mail:* mba@cob.sjsu.edu.

DEGREE & CERTIFICATE PROGRAMS

Master of Science in Transportation Management (MSTM)

In the fall of 1997 there were 9 students enrolled in this program.

Geographic service area/ restrictions Students must be matriculated at San Jose State University.

Application requirements *Prior education:* Baccalaureate degree. *Other requirements:* GMAT, college transcripts, an essay or personal statement, an application fee of $59.

Completion requirements 30 semester units. *Maximum time for completion:* seven years.

SHEFFIELD HALLAM UNIVERSITY

Sheffield Business School
Sheffield, United Kingdom

Sheffield Hallam University is a university in the United Kingdom. The Sheffield Business School first offered graduate business distance learning courses in 1993. In 1997–98, it offered 8 graduate business courses at a distance. In the fall of 1997, there were 600 students enrolled in distance learning graduate-level business courses and programs.

Course delivery sites Courses are delivered to 5 off-campus centers in Jersey (England), Bangalore (India), Hong Kong (China), Kuala Lumpur (Malaysia), Bahrain (Bahrain).

Media Courses are delivered via videoconferencing, computer conferencing, e-mail, print, director tutor contact (in-person for one course). Students and teachers may meet in person or interact via videoconferencing, mail, fax, e-mail. The following equipment may be required: a computer.

Geographic service area/ restrictions Programs are available worldwide. Students need to have appropriate work experience and the ability to attend an overseas location once per year.

Services Distance learners have access to library services, the campus computer network, e-mail services,

academic advising, tutoring, bookstore at a distance.

Credit-earning options Students may transfer credits from another institution or may earn credits through examinations, portfolio assessment.

Typical costs Tuition of $11,250 per degree program.

Registration Students may register by mail, fax, phone, e-mail, World Wide Web.

Contact J. Houghton, Postgraduate Business Admissions Officer, Sheffield Hallam University, BITC, Howard Street, Sheffield, S1 1WB, England. *Telephone:* 44-1142532820. *Fax:* 44-1142255268. *E-mail:* sbs. pgdinfo@shu.ac.uk. *Web site:* http:// www.shu.ac.uk/schools/sbs/.

DEGREE & CERTIFICATE PROGRAMS

Master of Business Administration (MBA)

In the fall of 1997 there were 400 students enrolled in this program.

Geographic service area/ restrictions Students must attend an overseas study center once per year.

Application requirements *Prior education:* a baccalaureate degree or the equivalent professional exam. *Other requirements:* college transcripts, letter(s) of recommendation, work experience.

Completion requirements 21 courses are required. *Maximum time for completion:* six years.

SOUTHERN ILLINOIS UNIVERSITY AT EDWARDSVILLE

School of Business
Edwardsville, Illinois

Southern Illinois University at Edwardsville, founded in 1957, is a state-supported comprehensive institution. It is accredited by the North Central Association of Colleges and Schools. The School of Business first offered graduate business distance learning courses in 1995. In 1997–98, it offered 7 graduate business courses at a distance. In the fall of 1997, there were 20 students enrolled in distance learning graduate-level business courses and programs.

Course delivery sites Courses are delivered to Kaskaskia College (Centralia), Rend Lake College (Ina).

Media Courses are delivered via interactive television. Students and teachers may interact via telephone, fax, e-mail, interactive television, World Wide Web.

Geographic service area/ restrictions Programs are available statewide. Students must be admitted to the MBA program.

Services Distance learners have access to e-mail services, academic advising, career placement assistance at a distance.

Credit-earning options Students may transfer credits from another institution.

Typical costs Tuition of $90.15 per semester hour plus mandatory fees of $16.80 per semester hour. Financial aid is available to distance learners.

Registration Students may register by phone, e-mail.

Contact Dr. Maurice Hirsch, Associate Dean, Southern Illinois University at Edwardsville, Box 1051, Edwardsville, IL 62026-1051. *Telephone:* 618-650-3412. *Fax:* 618-650-3979. *E-mail:* mhirsch@siue.edu. *Web site:* http://www.siue.edu/BUSINESS.

DEGREE & CERTIFICATE PROGRAMS

Master of Business Administration (MBA)

In the fall of 1997 there were 20 students enrolled in this program.

Geographic service area/restrictions Program is available locally.

Application requirements *Prior education:* Baccalaureate degree. *Other requirements:* GMAT, college transcripts, an application fee of $25.

Completion requirements 30–58 semester hours. *Maximum time for completion:* six years.

SOUTHWEST MISSOURI STATE UNIVERSITY

College of Business Administration
Springfield, Missouri

Southwest Missouri State University, founded in 1905, is a state-supported comprehensive institution. It is accredited by the North Central Association of Colleges and Schools. The College of Business Administration first offered graduate business distance learning courses in 1997. In 1997–98, it offered 12 graduate business courses at a distance. In the fall of 1997, there were 30 students enrolled in distance learning graduate-level business courses and programs.

Course delivery sites Students can receive instruction anywhere.

Media Courses are delivered via computer conferencing, World Wide Web, e-mail, print, on-campus residency (one week per semester). Students and teachers may interact via fax, e-mail. The following equipment may be required: a computer with access to the Internet and a frames-compatible web browser.

Geographic service area/ restrictions Programs are available nationwide. To enroll in MS CIS courses one must be an IT professional with at least two years of full-time work experience.

Services Distance learners have access to library services, the campus computer network, e-mail services at a distance.

Credit-earning options Students may transfer credits from another institution.

Typical costs Tuition of $2655 per semester for in-state residents. Tuition of $3555 per semester for out-of-state residents. Costs may vary by number of credits taken. Financial aid is available to distance learners.

Registration Students may register by mail, fax, phone, e-mail.

Contact Dr. David B. Meinert, Director, MS CIS Program, Southwest Missouri State University, CIS Department, 901 South National, Springfield, MO 65804. *Telephone:* 417-836-4131. *Fax:* 417-836-6907. *E-mail:* mscis@ mail.smsu.edu. *Web site:* http://www. mscis.smsu.edu.

DEGREE & CERTIFICATE PROGRAMS

Master of Science in Computer Information Systems (MSCIS)

In the fall of 1997 there were 30 students enrolled in this program.

Application requirements *Prior education:* a baccalaureate degree and at least nine hours of business courses and three computer courses. *Other requirements:* GMAT, college transcripts, an essay or personal statement, letter(s) of recommendation, an application fee of $25, students must be IT professionals with at least two years of full-time work experience.

Completion requirements 36 credit hours are required.

On-campus requirements Students must be on campus one week per semester.

STEPHENS COLLEGE

School of Graduate and Continuing Education

Columbia, Missouri

Stephens College, founded in 1833, is an independent-nonprofit comprehensive institution. It is accredited by the North Central Association of Colleges and Schools. The School of Graduate and Continuing Education first offered graduate business distance learning courses in 1997. In 1997–98, it offered 5 graduate business courses at a distance. In the fall of 1997, there were 7 students enrolled in distance learning graduate-level business courses and programs.

Course delivery sites Courses are delivered to your home, your workplace.

Media Courses are delivered via CD-ROM, World Wide Web, e-mail. Students and teachers may interact via mail, telephone, fax, e-mail. The following equipment may be required: a computer with a CD-ROM drive, access to the Internet, email, and spreadsheet software.

Geographic service area/ restrictions Programs are available worldwide. Students must have a minimum GPA of 3.0.

Services Distance learners have access to e-mail services, academic advising, career placement assistance, bookstore at a distance.

Credit-earning options Students may transfer credits from another institution or may earn credits through examinations, portfolio assessment, military training, business training.

Typical costs Tuition of $690 per course.

Registration Students may register by mail.

Contact Dr. Joan T. Rines, Director, Graduate and HIM Programs, Stephens College, Campus Box 2083, Columbia, MO 65215. *Telephone:* 573-876-7283. *Fax:* 573-876-7248. *E-mail:* grad@wc.stephens.edu. *Web site:* http://www.stephens.edu.

DEGREE & CERTIFICATE PROGRAMS

Master of Business Administration (MBA)

In the fall of 1997 there were 7 students enrolled in this program.

Application requirements *Prior education:* Baccalaureate degree. *Other requirements:* GMAT, TOEFL (for international applicants), college transcripts, an essay or personal statement, letter(s) of recommendation, an application fee of $25, a minimum GPA of 3.0, some students may need a personal interview.

Completion requirements 60 courses are required. *Maximum time for completion:* seven years.

On-campus requirements Students are required to complete a one-week capstone course on campus and a weekend orientation before starting the graduate program.

STRAYER UNIVERSITY

Strayer Online
Washington, District of Columbia

Strayer University, founded in 1892, is a proprietary comprehensive institution. It is accredited by the Middle States Association of Colleges and Schools. Strayer Online first offered graduate business distance learning courses in 1997. In 1997–98, it offered 40 graduate business courses at a distance. In the fall of 1997, there were 88 students enrolled in distance learning graduate-level business courses and programs.

Course delivery sites Students can receive instruction anywhere.

Media Courses are delivered via audioconferencing, World Wide Web, e-mail. Students and teachers may interact via audioconferencing, telephone, e-mail, World Wide Web. The following equipment may be required: a computer with access to the Internet and a sound card.

Geographic service area/ restrictions Programs are available nationwide.

Services Distance learners have access to library services, the campus computer network, e-mail services, academic advising, tutoring, career placement assistance, bookstore at a distance.

Credit-earning options Students may transfer credits from another institution.

Typical costs Tuition of $250 per quarter hour. Financial aid is available to distance learners.

Registration Students may register by mail, fax, phone, e-mail, World Wide Web.

Contact Mr. John Tucker, Director, Distance Learning, Strayer University, 8382-F Terminal Road, Lorton, VA 22079. *Telephone:* 703-339-1850. *Fax:* 703-339-1852. *E-mail:* jet@strayer. edu. *Web site:* http://www.strayer. edu.

DEGREE & CERTIFICATE PROGRAMS

Master of Science in Business Administration (MSBA)

In the fall of 1997 there were 88 students enrolled in this program.

Application requirements *Prior education:* Baccalaureate degree. *Other requirements:* GMAT or GRE, college transcripts, an application fee of $25, minimum undergraduate GPA of 2.75.

Completion requirements 54 quarter hour credits.

INDIVIDUAL COURSE SUBJECT AREAS

Graduate

Accounting; Business Communications; Economics; Financial Management/Planning; Information Management; Management Information Systems; Operations Management; Organizational Behavior/ Development; Quantitative Analysis; Strategic Management

SYRACUSE UNIVERSITY

School of Management

Syracuse, New York

Syracuse University, founded in 1870, is an independent-nonprofit university. It is accredited by the Middle States Association of Colleges and Schools. The School of Management first offered graduate business distance learning courses in 1971. In 1997–98, it offered 25 graduate business courses at a distance. In the fall of 1997, there were 100 students enrolled in distance learning graduate-level business courses and programs.

Course delivery sites Students can receive instruction anywhere.

Media Courses are delivered via World Wide Web, e-mail, print, one-week residencies for lectures. Students and teachers may meet in person or interact via mail, telephone, fax, e-mail, World Wide Web. The following equipment may be required: a computer with access to the Internet and email.

Geographic service area/restrictions Programs are available worldwide. Students must be admitted to the MBA program.

Services Distance learners have access to library services, the campus computer network, e-mail services, academic advising, career placement assistance, course-specific discussion rooms at a distance.

Credit-earning options Students may transfer credits from another institution or may earn credits through examinations, portfolio assessment.

Typical costs Tuition of $555 per credit. Financial aid is available to distance learners.

Registration Students may register by mail.

Contact Paula Charland, Assistant Dean, Syracuse University, 100 Crouse-Hinds School of Management Building, 900 South Crouse Avenue, Syracuse, NY 13244-2130. *Telephone:* 315-443-9214. *Fax:* 315-443-9517. *E-mail:* mbainfo@som.syr.edu. *Web site:* http://sominfo.syr.edu.

DEGREE & CERTIFICATE PROGRAMS

Master of Business Administration (MBA)

In the fall of 1997 there were 100 students enrolled in this program.

In 1996–97, 25 degrees were earned at a distance through this program.

Application requirements *Prior education:* Baccalaureate degree. *Other requirements:* GMAT, TOEFL (for international applicants), college transcripts, an essay or personal statement, letter(s) of recommendation, an application fee of $40, work experience.

Completion requirements 54 credits are required. *Maximum time for completion:* seven years.

On-campus requirements Students must attend one-week residencies three times a year.

SYRACUSE UNIVERSITY

SCHOOL OF MANAGEMENT
S Y R A C U S E

School of Management

Independent Study M.B.A. Program
Syracuse, New York

THE UNIVERSITY

Established in 1870, Syracuse University is one of the oldest and most comprehensive independent universities in the United States. The School of Management, founded in 1919, was the first collegiate business school in New York State (outside of New York City) and the sixteenth in the nation to be accredited by the AACSB–The International Association for Management Education. The School's M.B.A. program, established in 1948, has been ranked consistently among the top fifty M.B.A. programs in the United States. M.B.A. programs are offered in full-time, part-time, executive, and independent study formats. Offered since 1977, the Independent Study M.B.A. is a pioneer distance learning program.

DISTANCE LEARNING PROGRAM

The Independent Study M.B.A. is a limited-residency distance education program. It is designed to meet the needs of accomplished professionals worldwide who want to acquire an accredited degree without interrupting their careers. Each semester begins with a required weeklong residency on Syracuse University's campus in beautiful upstate New York. Students meet at residencies three times each year, in January, May, and August. During the residencies, students attend classes that serve to orient them to the demands and expectations of the curriculum. Students also establish bonds and working relationships with faculty members and fellow students. Following the residency, students return to their homes with a clear understanding of the work requirements of the semester and access to the resources necessary for successful completion of their courses. The program enrolls students from many states and other countries who represent numerous prominent corporations and government agencies.

DELIVERY MEDIA

The program is delivered in three annual on-campus residencies. Between the weeklong residencies, the Internet is used by most faculty members to enrich the independent study learning experience. Faculty members post assignments and cases to the Internet for downloading by students. Some create listservs or chat rooms for increased communication between the students and faculty members and among students. Students find that basic computer and Internet skills are advantageous for deriving the most from this program. Entering students are expected to have access to at least a 486 computer (Pentium preferred), a 14.4k-baud modem, and a fax machine.

SPECIAL PROGRAMS
In addition to the three yearly on-campus residencies, Independent Study M.B.A. courses are also offered occasionally at optional off-campus residencies. In 1998–99, the University plans to offer off-campus residencies in Shanghai, China, and in London, England.

FACULTY
The independent study faculty members are the same terminal degree–bearing faculty members who teach in the full-time and part-time M.B.A. programs at Syracuse. They often cite the independent study program as their favorite teaching experience because of the diversity and sophistication of the students who are attracted to the program.

STUDENT SERVICES
Academic advising is provided in person during each of the on-campus residencies as well as year-round through e-mail and fax correspondence. Career advisement is available for independent study students through the School of Management Career Center.

CREDIT OPTIONS
The Independent Study M.B.A. emphasizes a broad, strategic-management view of business. The curriculum consists of 54 credits of course work. The normal course load is 6

credits per semester. Students typically finish the program within three years. Under certain circumstances, up to 6 credits of course work may be transferred into the program from other institutions, and up to 18 credits of course work may be waived.

ADMISSION
Admission is very competitive. It is based on an evaluation of the applicant's undergraduate work, professional experience, essays, recommendations, and performance on the Graduate Management Admission Test (GMAT). The Test of English as a Foreign Language (TOEFL) is required of international applicants whose native language is not English.

TUITION AND FEES
Tuition for 1998–99 is $555 per credit. There are no additional fees beyond the $40 application fee. The average cost for housing during the on-campus residencies ranges from $52 to $99 per day, depending on the choice of accommodations.

FINANCIAL AID
Institutional financial aid is not available for students in this program. Most students hold a full or partial sponsorship from their employers. Loan programs may be available in some circumstances.

APPLYING
Applicants must submit their completed application, including test scores, at least six weeks prior to the start date of the residency they wish to attend. Students must be matricu-

lated in the M.B.A. program before they enroll for classes.

CONTACT

Paula A. Charland, Assistant Dean
M.B.A. and Master's Admissions
  Office
School of Management
Suite 100

Syracuse University
Syracuse, New York 13244-2130
Telephone: 315-443-9214
Fax: 315-443-9517
E-mail: mbainfo@som.syr.edu
Web site: http://sominfo.syr.edu
  http://MBA.CollegeEdge.
  com (for online applica-
  tion)

TEMPLE UNIVERSITY
School of Business and Management–MBA Program
Philadelphia, Pennsylvania

Temple University, founded in 1884, is a state-related university. It is accredited by the Middle States Association of Colleges and Schools. The School of Business and Management first offered graduate business distance learning courses in 1996. In 1997–98, it offered 14 graduate business courses at a distance. In the fall of 1997, there were 50 students enrolled in distance learning graduate-level business courses and programs.

Course delivery sites Courses are delivered to your home, 1 off-campus center in Harrisburg.

Media Courses are delivered via videoconferencing, World Wide Web, e-mail. Students and teachers may meet in person or interact via videoconferencing, telephone, e-mail. The following equipment may be required: a computer with access to the Internet and email for online courses.

Geographic service area/restrictions Video courses are site-specific while online courses are available worldwide. Students must meet the School of Business' minimum academic standards.

Services Distance learners have access to library services, the campus computer network, e-mail services, academic advising, career placement assistance at a distance.

Credit-earning options Students may earn credits through examinations. Financial aid is available to distance learners.

Registration Students may register by fax, phone.

Contact Linda J. Whelan, Director MBA and MS Programs, Temple University, Speakman Hall, Room 5, 1810 North 13th Street, Philadelphia, PA 19122. *Telephone:* 215-204-4563. *Fax:* 215-204-8300. *E-mail:* linda@ sbm.temple.edu. *Web site:* http:// www.sbm.temple.edu.

INDIVIDUAL COURSE SUBJECT AREAS

Graduate
Accounting; Economics; Finance; Operations Management

THOMAS EDISON STATE COLLEGE

Office of Graduate Studies
Trenton, New Jersey

Thomas Edison State College, founded in 1972, is a state-supported comprehensive institution. It is accredited by the Middle States Association of Colleges and Schools. The Office of Graduate Studies first offered graduate business distance learning courses in 1996. In 1997–98, it offered 10 graduate business courses at a distance. In the fall of 1997, there were 49 students enrolled in distance learning graduate-level business courses and programs.

Course delivery sites Students can receive instruction anywhere.

Media Courses are delivered via World Wide Web, e-mail, print. Students and teachers may interact via mail, telephone, fax, e-mail, World Wide Web. The following equipment may be required: a computer (486 or better), 8MB of RAM, 20MB of available disk space, a 14.4K modem, Netscape 3.01 (or another Internet browser), and email.

Geographic service area/ restrictions Programs are available nationwide. Applicants are expected to have a baccalaureate degree and at least three years experience in positions with significant supervisory, technical, or administrative responsibilities.

Services Distance learners have access to library services, the campus computer network, academic advising, bookstore at a distance.

Credit-earning options Students may transfer credits from another institution or may earn credits through military training, business training.

Typical costs Tuition of $289 per credit. Financial aid is available to distance learners.

Registration Students may register by mail, fax.

Contact Dr. Esther Taitsman, Associate Dean and Director of Graduate Studies, Thomas Edison State College, 101 West State Street, Trenton, NJ 08608-1176. *Telephone:* 609-292-5143. *Fax:* 609-777-2956. *E-mail:* msm@call.tesc.edu. *Web site:* http://www.tesc.edu.

MBA–Distance Learning Programs

DEGREE & CERTIFICATE PROGRAMS

Master of Science (MS)

In the fall of 1997 there were 49 students enrolled in this program.

Application requirements *Prior education:* Baccalaureate degree. *Other requirements:* college transcripts, an essay or personal statement, letter(s) of recommendation, an application fee of $75, work experience, at least three years experience in positions with significant supervisory, technical or administrative responsibilities.

Completion requirements 36 credits are required.

On-campus requirements Students must be on campus for two weekends, one at the beginning and one at the end of the program.

THUNDERBIRD, THE AMERICAN GRADUATE SCHOOL OF INTERNATIONAL MANAGEMENT

Master of International Management in Latin America Program

Glendale, Arizona

Thunderbird, The American Graduate School of International Management is an independent-nonprofit graduate institution. It is accredited by the North Central Association of Colleges and Schools. The Master of International Management in Latin America Program first offered graduate business distance learning courses in 1998. In 1997–98, it offered 20 graduate business courses at a distance.

Course delivery sites Courses are delivered to ITESM campuses throughout Mexico.

Media Courses are delivered via videoconferencing, computer software, CD-ROM, computer conferencing, World Wide Web, e-mail. Students and teachers may interact via videoconferencing, e-mail, interactive television, World Wide Web. The following equipment may be required: a computer with access to the Internet.

Geographic service area/restrictions Programs are currently limited to Mexico, but will soon include sites in Argentina, Chile, and South America.

Services Distance learners have access to library services, e-mail services, career placement assistance, bookstore at a distance.

Typical costs Tuition of $10,000 per year plus mandatory fees of $500 per year. Financial aid is available to distance learners.

Registration Students may register by mail, fax, phone, e-mail, World Wide Web.

Contact Judy Johnson, Assistant Vice President for Admissions and Recruiting, Thunderbird, The American Graduate School of International Management, Thunderbird Campus— Admissions, 15249 North 59th Avenue, Glendale, AZ 85306. *Telephone:* 602-978-7210. *Fax:* 602-439-5432. *E-mail:* t-bird@t-bird.edu.

DEGREE & CERTIFICATE PROGRAMS

Master of International Management in Latin America (MIMLA)

Geographic service area/ restrictions Program is available in Latin America.

Application requirements *Prior education:* Baccalaureate degree. *Other requirements:* GMAT, TOEFL (for international applicants), letter(s) of recommendation, resume, copy of birth certificate.

Completion requirements 50 semester credit hours. *Maximum time for completion:* five years.

On-campus requirements The program begins with one week on the Thunderbird campus and ends with one week on the ITESM campus in Monterrey, Mexico.

UNIVERSITÉ DE MONCTON

Moncton, New Brunswick, Canada

Université de Moncton, founded in 1963, is a province-supported comprehensive institution. It is provincially chartered. It first offered graduate business distance learning courses in 1995. In 1997–98, it offered 7 graduate business courses at a distance. In the fall of 1997, there were 100 students enrolled in distance learning graduate-level business courses and programs.

Course delivery sites Courses are delivered to your home, 6 off-campus centers in Bathurst, Campbellton, Edmundston, La Butte, Moncton, Shippagan.

Media Courses are delivered via videoconferencing, World Wide Web, e-mail. Students and teachers may meet in person or interact via videoconferencing, mail, telephone, fax, e-mail, World Wide Web. The following equipment may be required: a computer with access to the Internet.

Geographic service area/ restrictions Programs are available nationwide.

Services Distance learners have access to library services, e-mail services, bookstore at a distance.

Credit-earning options Students may transfer credits from another institution or may earn credits through examinations, portfolio assessment.

Typical costs Tuition of $110 per credit for in-state residents. Tuition of $200 per credit for out-of-state residents. Tuition is in Canadian dollars.

Registration Students may register by mail, fax, phone.

Contact Charles Antoine le Blanc, Associate Director, Université de Moncton, Education Permanente, Moncton, NB E1A 3E9, Canada. *Telephone:* 506-858-4121. *Fax:* 506-858-4489. *E-mail:* blancha@umoncton. ca. *Web site:* http://www.umoncton. ca/educ-perm/eduperm.html.

DEGREE & CERTIFICATE PROGRAMS

Master of Business Administration (MBA)

In the fall of 1997 there were 50 students enrolled in this program.

Application requirements *Prior education:* Baccalaureate degree. *Other*

requirements: college transcripts, letter(s) of recommendation, work experience.

Completion requirements 45 credits are required. *Maximum time for completion:* seven years.

INDIVIDUAL COURSE SUBJECT AREAS

Graduate

Accounting; Finance; Management; Marketing

THE UNIVERSITY OF AKRON

Graduate Programs in Business
Akron, Ohio

The University of Akron, founded in 1870, is a state-supported university. It is accredited by the North Central Association of Colleges and Schools. The Graduate Programs in Business first offered graduate business distance learning courses in 1998.

Course delivery sites Students can receive instruction anywhere.

Media Courses are delivered via CD-ROM, computer conferencing, World Wide Web, e-mail. Students and teachers may interact via telephone, fax, e-mail, World Wide Web. The following equipment may be required: a multimedia computer with a CD-ROM drive, a modem, and access to the Internet.

Geographic service area/ restrictions Programs are available worldwide. Students must be registered with the university.

Services Distance learners have access to library services, the campus computer network, e-mail services, academic advising, career placement assistance at a distance.

Typical costs Tuition of $164.85 per semester credit plus mandatory fees of $6.30 per semester credit for in-state residents. Tuition of $308.15 per semester credit plus mandatory fees of $6.30 per semester credit for out-of-state residents. Financial aid is available to distance learners.

Registration Students may register by phone.

Contact Dr. J. Daniel Williams, Associate Dean and Director, The University of Akron, 259 South Broadway, Room 412, Akron, OH 44325-4805. *Telephone:* 330-972-7043. *Fax:* 330-972-6588. *E-mail:* jwilliams@uakron.edu. *Web site:* http://www.uakron.edu/cba/.

DEGREE & CERTIFICATE PROGRAMS

Master of Business Administration (MBA)

In the fall of 1997 there were 552 students enrolled in this program.

Geographic service area/ restrictions Program is available in regional area only.

Application requirements *Prior education:* Baccalaureate degree. *Other requirements:* GMAT, college

transcripts, an application fee of $25 for US students, $50 for international students.

Completion requirements 34–58 semester credits. *Maximum time for completion:* six years.

On-campus requirements Students make three visits to campus each semester for orientation, midterm, and final examinations.

UNIVERSITY OF ARKANSAS AT LITTLE ROCK

College of Business Administration
Little Rock, Arkansas

University of Arkansas at Little Rock, founded in 1927, is a state-supported university. It is accredited by the North Central Association of Colleges and Schools. The College of Business Administration first offered graduate business distance learning courses in 1997. In 1997–98, it offered 7 graduate business courses at a distance. In the fall of 1997, there were 30 students enrolled in distance learning graduate-level business courses and programs.

Course delivery sites Courses are delivered to Southern Arkansas University–Magnolia (Magnolia), University of Arkansas at Monticello (Monticello).

Media Courses are delivered via videoconferencing, interactive television, e-mail. Students and teachers may meet in person or interact via videoconferencing, mail, fax, e-mail, interactive television.

Geographic service area/restrictions Programs are available statewide. Students must meet the program entrance requirements.

Services Distance learners have access to library services, e-mail services at a distance.

Credit-earning options Students may transfer credits from another institution or may earn credits through examinations.

Typical costs Tuition of $130 per credit plus mandatory fees of $11.50 per credit for in-state residents. Tuition of $278 per credit plus mandatory fees of $11.50 per credit for out-of-state residents. Financial aid is available to distance learners.

Registration Students may register by e-mail.

Contact Tammy Lawrence, MBA Coordinator, University of Arkansas at Little Rock, College of Business Administration, 2801 South University Avenue, Little Rock, AR 72204. *Telephone:* 501-569-3391. *Fax:* 501-

569-8898. *E-mail:* talawrence@ualr. edu. *Web site:* http://www.ualr.edu.

DEGREE & CERTIFICATE PROGRAMS

Master of Business Administration (MBA)

In the fall of 1997 there were 30 students enrolled in this program.

Application requirements *Prior education:* Baccalaureate degree. *Other requirements:* GMAT, college transcripts.

Completion requirements 30 semester credit hours.

UNIVERSITY OF BALTIMORE

Merrick School of Business

Baltimore, Maryland

University of Baltimore, founded in 1925, is a state-supported upper-level institution. It is accredited by the Middle States Association of Colleges and Schools. The Merrick School of Business first offered graduate business distance learning courses in 1997.

Course delivery sites Courses are delivered to your home, 1 off-campus center in Hartford.

Media Courses are delivered via televison, videotapes, interactive television, computer software, World Wide Web, e-mail, print. Students and teachers may interact via telephone, interactive television. The following equipment may be required: a computer with access to the Internet for web-based courses.

Geographic service area/restrictions Programs are available statewide.

Services Distance learners have access to library services, e-mail services, bookstore at a distance.

Typical costs Tuition of $1200 per course. Financial aid is available to distance learners.

Registration Students may register by mail, fax, phone.

Contact Daniel A. Gerlowski, Associate Dean, University of Baltimore, 1420 North Charles Street, Baltimore, MD 21201. *Telephone:* 410-837-4987. *Fax:* 410-837-5652. *E-mail:* dgerlowski@ubmail.ubalt.edu.

DEGREE & CERTIFICATE PROGRAMS

Master of Business Administration (MBA)

Application requirements *Prior education:* Baccalaureate degree. *Other requirements:* GMAT, college transcripts, an essay or personal statement, letter(s) of recommendation, an application fee of $35.

Completion requirements 48 credits are required.

INDIVIDUAL COURSE SUBJECT AREAS

Graduate
Economics; Management

UNIVERSITY OF COLORADO AT COLORADO SPRINGS

Graduate School of Business Administration
Colorado Springs, Colorado

University of Colorado at Colorado Springs, founded in 1965, is a state-supported comprehensive institution. It is accredited by the North Central Association of Colleges and Schools. The Graduate School of Business Administration first offered graduate business distance learning courses in 1996. In 1997–98, it offered 15 graduate business courses at a distance. In the fall of 1997, there were 151 students enrolled in distance learning graduate-level business courses and programs.

Course delivery sites Courses are delivered to your home.

Media Courses are delivered via television, videotapes, World Wide Web, e-mail. Students and teachers may interact via mail, telephone, e-mail, World Wide Web. The following equipment may be required: a TV and a VCR and/or an IBM computer (486 or better) or the MAC equivalent, with a 14.4K modem, access to the Internet, and email.

Geographic service area/ restrictions Programs are available worldwide.

Services Distance learners have access to academic advising at a distance.

Credit-earning options Students may earn credits through examinations.

Typical costs Tuition of $750 per course.

Registration Students may register by mail, fax, phone, e-mail.

Contact Barbara Neiberg, MBA Program Director, University of Colorado at Colorado Springs, 1420 Austin Bluffs Parkway, PO Box 7150, Colorado Springs, CO 80933. *Telephone:* 719-262-3401. *Fax:* 719-262-3494. *E-mail:* bneiberg@mail. uccs.edu. *Web site:* http://www.uccs. edu/~collbus.

DEGREE & CERTIFICATE PROGRAMS

Master of Business Administration (MBA)

In the fall of 1997 there were 100 students enrolled in this program.

Application requirements *Prior education:* Baccalaureate degree. *Other requirements:* GMAT, college transcripts, an application fee of $65 for US students, $75 for international students.

Completion requirements 36 credit hours are required. *Maximum time for completion:* five years.

INDIVIDUAL COURSE SUBJECT AREAS

Graduate

Accounting; Finance; International Business; Management; Management Information Systems; Marketing; Operations Management; Production Management

UNIVERSITY OF COLORADO AT COLORADO SPRINGS

Graduate School of Business Administration

Distance M.B.A. Degree
Colorado Springs, Colorado

THE COLLEGE

The University of Colorado at Colorado Springs (CU–Colorado Springs) is located on a 470-acre campus in northeast Colorado Springs at the foot of Austin Bluffs, with a sweeping view of the Front Range of the Rocky Mountains. A gift of the Cragmor Foundation to the University, the campus, then 80 acres, opened for classes in 1965. CU–Colorado Springs is a full-service university that offers programs that lead to twenty-four bachelor's degrees, fifteen master's degrees, and two doctorates. The College of Business is dedicated to leadership and excellence in business education, intellectual contributions, and service. Consistent with the policies of the University of Colorado and in recognition of its many and varied constituents, the College of Business maintains a traditional, balanced emphasis on each of these activities. The College of Business has earned accreditation from AACSB–The International Association for Management Education, the most prestigious accreditation a business school can earn.

DISTANCE LEARNING PROGRAM

The College of Business offers an M.B.A. degree in cooperation with Jones Education Company's (JEC) College Connection. This program consists of 36 hours of course work that is delivered through a combination of video presentation, Internet-based materials, and required communication among students and faculty members. Students may be required to take up to 15 hours of pre-M.B.A. preparatory course work, depending on their educational background and the year their undergraduate course work was completed. Students who graduate from the distance program earn the same degree as students who attend the CU–Colorado Springs campus and work with the same faculty on a curriculum designed specifically for busy, working adults.

DELIVERY MEDIA

Technology requirements are as follows: 486 or Pentium (preferred) PC or comparable Macintosh computer, 28.8 KBPS or faster modem, access to the Internet (preferably a connection through a local Internet service provider—also known as an ISP), an up-to-date World Wide Web browser

(Netscape Navigator version 3.01 or later preferred), and an e-mail account.

FACULTY

Faculty members at CU–Colorado Springs instill excitement about learning that translates into effective results at work. Nearly all courses are taught by full-time, doctorally qualified faculty members from nationally recognized universities. The learning experience is enriched by the faculty's efforts in leading-edge research, academic publishing, community involvement, and organizational consulting. CU–Colorado Springs offers professional instruction in highly interactive M.B.A. classes.

CREDIT OPTIONS

The M.B.A. program may accept a maximum of 6 hours of transfer credit from another M.B.A. program that is accredited by AACSB–The International Association for Management Education.

ADMISSION

In order to be considered for admission, applicants must submit the following: the CU–Colorado Springs application package with accompanying fee, official transcripts from all institutions attended, a bachelor's degree from a regionally accredited university, acceptable GMAT scores, three letters of recommendation, and a current resume. International students must submit a TOEFL score of at least 550 for the paper-based exam or at least 213 for the computer-based exam.

TUITION AND FEES

Tuition is $825 per course. Fees, books, materials, and shipping costs are additional.

FINANCIAL AID

Financial aid is available through P.L.A.T.O., a loan program for undergraduate and graduate students. To receive a P.L.A.T.O. brochure, students should contact JEC College Connection. The CU–Colorado Springs M.B.A. is approved for veterans' educational benefits. Qualified students should contact the CU–Colorado Springs Veterans Affairs Office by e-mail at vacert@mail.uccs.edu.

APPLYING

Admission is primarily based on a combination of the grade point average from the applicant's undergraduate program and the results from the GMAT. Admission issues are directed to the MBA Advising Office at CU–Colorado Springs, while enrollment is accomplished by contacting JEC College Connection.

CONTACT

Education Services Center
JEC College Connection
9697 East Mineral Avenue
Englewood, Colorado 80155-6612
Telephone: 800-777-MIND (toll-free)
Fax: 303-799-0966
E-mail: edcenter@jec.edu
Web site: http://www.jec.edu

MBA Advising (Distance Education Office)
College of Business

University of Colorado at Colorado Springs
P.O. Box 7150
Colorado Springs, Colorado 80933-7150

Telephone: 800-990-8227 Ext. 3070 (toll-free)
Fax: 719-262-3100
E-mail: ksangerm@mail.uccs.edu
Web site: http://www.uccs.edu

UNIVERSITY OF COLORADO AT DENVER

Graduate College of Business

Denver, Colorado

University of Colorado at Denver, founded in 1912, is a state-supported university. It is accredited by the North Central Association of Colleges and Schools. The Graduate College of Business first offered graduate business distance learning courses in 1998. In 1997–98, it offered 6 graduate business courses at a distance.

Course delivery sites Students can receive instruction anywhere.

Media Courses are delivered via World Wide Web. Students and teachers may interact via e-mail, World Wide Web. The following equipment may be required: a computer (486 or better) with Windows 3.1 or 95 or Mac OS, Java, email, a Real Player, a 14.4K modem (or faster), and an Internet Service Provider.

Geographic service area/restrictions Programs are available worldwide. Class size is restricted to 45. Online students must be registered as graduate business students.

Services Distance learners have access to library services, the campus computer network, e-mail services, academic advising, bookstore at a distance.

Typical costs Tuition of $222 per credit hour plus mandatory fees of $150 per semester for in-state residents. Tuition of $752 per credit hour for out-of-state residents. Financial aid is available to distance learners.

Registration Students may register by phone, World Wide Web.

Contact Teri Burleson, Graduate Advisor and CU Online Coordinator, University of Colorado at Denver, Campus Box 165, PO Box 173364, Denver, CO 80217. *Telephone:* 303-556-6517. *Fax:* 303-556-5904. *E-mail:* teri_burleson@maroon.cudenver.edu.

INDIVIDUAL COURSE SUBJECT AREAS

Graduate
Accounting; Business Information Science; Financial Management/Planning

UNIVERSITY OF DALLAS
Graduate School of Management
Irving, Texas

University of Dallas, founded in 1955, is an independent-religious Roman Catholic university. It is accredited by the Southern Association of Colleges and Schools. The Graduate School of Management first offered graduate business distance learning courses in 1994. In 1997–98, it offered 6 graduate business courses at a distance. In the fall of 1997, there were 85 students enrolled in distance learning graduate-level business courses and programs.

Course delivery sites Courses are delivered to hospitals, Westcott Health Sciences Network–Long Term Care Network.

Media Courses are delivered via television, videotapes, videoconferencing, interactive television, e-mail. Students and teachers may meet in person or interact via mail, telephone, fax, e-mail, interactive television.

Geographic service area/restrictions Programs are available nationwide. Students must be employed by a subscriber hospital.

Services Distance learners have access to e-mail services, academic advising, bookstore at a distance.

Credit-earning options Students may earn credits through examinations.

Typical costs Tuition of $885 per course. Financial aid is available to distance learners.

Registration Students may register by mail, fax, phone, e-mail.

Contact Roger Carruth, Distance Learning Coordinator, University of Dallas, 1845 East Northgate Drive, Irving, TX 75062. *Telephone:* 972-721-5174. *Fax:* 972-721-4009.

DEGREE & CERTIFICATE PROGRAMS

Master of Business Administration (MBA)

In the fall of 1997 there were 85 students enrolled in this program. In 1996–97, 36 degrees were earned at a distance through this program.

Geographic service area/restrictions Students must be employed by a subscriber hospital.

Application requirements *Prior education:* Baccalaureate degree. *Other requirements:* GMAT, college

transcripts, letter(s) of recommendation, work experience.

Completion requirements 49 credit
hours are required. *Maximum time
for completion:* six years.

UNIVERSITY OF FLORIDA

Warrington College of Business Administration

Gainesville, Florida

University of Florida, founded in 1853, is a state-supported university. It is accredited by the Southern Association of Colleges and Schools.

Course delivery sites Students can receive instruction anywhere.

Media Courses are delivered via videoconferencing, audioconferencing, computer software, CD-ROM, computer conferencing, World Wide Web, e-mail, print. Students and teachers may meet in person or interact via videoconferencing, audioconferencing, mail, telephone, fax, e-mail, World Wide Web. The following equipment may be required: a laptop computer (at least 200MHz) with 64 MB of RAM, 2 GB of hard drive space, an 8x CD-ROM drive, Windows 95, MS Office 97, a modem and a camera.

Geographic service area/restrictions Programs are available worldwide. Students must be formally admitted into the degree program.

Services Distance learners have access to library services, the campus computer network, e-mail services, academic advising, career placement assistance at a distance.

Credit-earning options Students may earn credits through examinations.

Typical costs Tuition of $29,500 per degree program. Financial aid is available to distance learners.

Registration Students may register by mail, fax, phone, e-mail, World Wide Web.

Contact Todd Reale, Director, Admissions and Marketing, University of Florida, PO Box 117152, 134 Bryan Hall, Gainesville, FL 32611-7152. *Telephone:* 352-392-7992. *Fax:* 352-392-8791. *E-mail:* treale@notes.cba. ufl.edu. *Web site:* http://www.cba.ufl. edu/mba.

DEGREE & CERTIFICATE PROGRAMS

Master of Business Administration (MBA)

Application requirements *Prior education:* Baccalaureate degree. *Other requirements:* GMAT, college transcripts, an essay or personal statement, letter(s) of recommendation, an application fee of $20, work experience, interview.

Completion requirements 48 semester credits are required. *Other requirements:* students take a one-week European trip during the fourth term. *Maximum time for completion:* twenty months.

On-campus requirements Students are on campus for a three-day weekend at the end of each term to take final exams, make presentations, and meet the faculty for the subsequent term.

UNIVERSITY OF GUELPH
MBA in Agriculture Program
Guelph, Ontario, Canada

University of Guelph, founded in 1964, is a province-supported university. It is accredited by the American Society of Landscape Architects. The MBA in Agriculture Program first offered graduate business distance learning courses in 1997. In 1997–98, it offered 5 graduate business courses at a distance. In the fall of 1997, there were 35 students enrolled in distance learning graduate-level business courses and programs.

Course delivery sites Students can receive instruction anywhere.

Media Courses are delivered via computer software. Students and teachers may interact via Lotus Notes. The following equipment may be required: a computer with a Pentium processor, a CD-ROM drive, 1 GB of hard drive space, 16 MB of RAM, and Windows 95 or NT. The school provides students with Lotus Notes and MS Office software.

Geographic service area/restrictions Programs are available worldwide. Students must be admitted into the degree program.

Services Distance learners have access to library services, the campus computer network, e-mail services, bookstore at a distance.

Typical costs Tuition of $1500 per course. Tuition in Canadian dollars. Additional charges may be required for international delivery.

Registration Students may register by mail, fax, phone, e-mail.

Contact Dr. Tom Funk, Director, MBA in Agriculture, University of Guelph, Room 221, MacLachlan Building, Guelph, ON N1G 2W1, Canada. *Telephone:* 888-MBA-AGRI. *Fax:* 519-767-1510. *E-mail:* mbaagri@uoguelph.ca. *Web site:* http://www.mbaagri.uoguelph.ca.

DEGREE & CERTIFICATE PROGRAMS

Master of Business Administration (MBA)

In the fall of 1997 there were 35 students enrolled in this program.

Geographic service area/restrictions Students without a baccalaureate degree must apply for special candidacy which requires approximately ten years of managerial experience in agribusiness.

University of Guelph

Application requirements *Prior education:* Baccalaureate degree. *Other requirements:* college transcripts, an essay or personal statement, letter(s) of recommendation, an application fee of $100 Canadian dollars, work experience, resume.

Completion requirements 11 courses are required. *Other requirements:* students must complete a project-based research paper. *Maximum time for completion:* six years.

On-campus requirements Students must complete a seven-day summer residency.

MBA–Distance Learning Programs

UNIVERSITY OF ILLINOIS AT SPRINGFIELD

Springfield, Illinois

University of Illinois at Springfield, founded in 1969, is a state-supported upper-level institution. It is accredited by the North Central Association of Colleges and Schools.

Course delivery sites Students can receive instruction anywhere.

Media Courses are delivered via computer conferencing, World Wide Web, e-mail. Students and teachers may meet in person or interact via audioconferencing, mail, telephone, fax, e-mail, World Wide Web. The following equipment may be required: a computer with access to the Internet and a high speed modem.

Geographic service area/ restrictions Programs are available statewide. Students must have a bachelor's degree.

Services Distance learners have access to library services, the campus computer network, e-mail services, academic advising, career placement assistance, bookstore at a distance.

Typical costs Tuition of $93 per credit hour for in-state residents. Tuition of $280 per credit hour for out-of-state residents. Financial aid is available to distance learners.

Registration Students may register by phone.

Contact Rassule Hadidi, Chair, Department of Management Information Systems, University of Illinois at Springfield, PO Box 19243, Springfield, IL 62794-9243. *Telephone:* 217-206-6067. *Fax:* 217-206-7543. *E-mail:* hadidi.rassule@uis.edu.

DEGREE & CERTIFICATE PROGRAMS

Master of Arts (MA)

Application requirements *Prior education:* Baccalaureate degree. *Other requirements:* GMAT or GRE, college transcripts, two semesters of accounting, one semester of production/operations management, one semester of statistics, one semester of college algebra or mathematics, computer in structured programming language.

Completion requirements 44 semester credit hours. *Maximum time for completion:* six years.

On-campus requirements Students must be on campus for presentations.

UNIVERSITY OF MARYLAND UNIVERSITY COLLEGE

Graduate School of Management and Technology

College Park, Maryland

University of Maryland University College, founded in 1947, is a state-supported comprehensive institution. It is accredited by the Middle States Association of Colleges and Schools. The Graduate School of Management and Technology first offered graduate business distance learning courses in 1982. In 1997–98, it offered 40 graduate business courses at a distance. In the fall of 1997, there were 509 students enrolled in distance learning graduate-level business courses and programs.

Course delivery sites Courses are delivered to your home, your workplace, military bases, 6 off-campus centers in Aberdeen, Annapolis, Baltimore, Patuxent River, Rockville, Waldorf.

Media Courses are delivered via videoconferencing, interactive television, computer conferencing, World Wide Web. Students and teachers may interact via videoconferencing, mail, telephone, fax, e-mail, interactive television, World Wide Web. The following equipment may be required: a computer (486 or better) with an Internet Service Provider, a web browser, a 28.8K modem, and email.

Geographic service area/restrictions Programs are available worldwide.

Services Distance learners have access to library services, the campus computer network, e-mail services, academic advising, bookstore at a distance.

Credit-earning options Students may transfer credits from another institution or may earn credits through military training, business training.

Typical costs Tuition of $273 per credit for in-state residents. Tuition of $353 per credit for out-of-state residents. *Non-credit courses:* $250 per course. Financial aid is available to distance learners.

Registration Students may register by mail, fax, e-mail, World Wide Web.

Contact Coordinator, Graduate Student Services, University of Maryland University College, Graduate Admissions and Advising, University Boulevard at Adelphi Road, College Park, MD 20742. *Telephone:* 301-985-7155. *Fax:* 301-985-7175. *E-mail:* gradinfo@nova.umuc.edu. *Web site:* http://www.umuc.edu.

DEGREE & CERTIFICATE PROGRAMS

Master in Management (MIM)

Application requirements *Prior education:* Baccalaureate degree. *Other requirements:* college transcripts, an essay or personal statement, an application fee of $50.

Completion requirements 36–39 semester hours. *Maximum time for completion:* seven years.

Master of General Administration (MGA)

Application requirements *Prior education:* Baccalaureate degree. *Other requirements:* college transcripts, an essay or personal statement, an application fee of $50.

Completion requirements 36–39 semester hours. *Maximum time for completion:* seven years.

Master of Science (MS)

Application requirements *Prior education:* Baccalaureate degree. *Other requirements:* college transcripts, an essay or personal statement, an application fee of $50.

Completion requirements 36–39 semester hours. *Maximum time for completion:* seven years.

UNIVERSITY OF MISSOURI–KANSAS CITY

Henry W. Bloch School of Business and Public Administration

Kansas City, Missouri

University of Missouri–Kansas City, founded in 1929, is a state-supported university. It is accredited by the North Central Association of Colleges and Schools. The Henry W. Bloch School of Business and Public Administration first offered graduate business distance learning courses in 1996. In the fall of 1997, there were 35 students enrolled in distance learning graduate-level business courses and programs.

Course delivery sites Courses are delivered to Inti College (Kuala Lumpur, Malaysia).

Media Courses are delivered via computer software, e-mail, fax. Students and teachers may meet in person or interact via mail, fax, e-mail, World Wide Web.

Geographic service area/restrictions Programs are available worldwide. Students must have an undergraduate degree.

Services Distance learners have access to e-mail services, academic advising, tutoring at a distance.

Typical costs Tuition of $17,200 per degree program.

Contact William Eddy, Dean, University of Missouri–Kansas City, 5100 Rockhill Road, Kansas City, MO 64110. *Telephone:* 816-235-1012.

Fax: 816-235-2206. *E-mail:* wbeddy@cctr.umkc.edu.

DEGREE & CERTIFICATE PROGRAMS

Executive Master of Business Administration (EMBA)

In the fall of 1997 there were 35 students enrolled in this program.

Geographic service area/restrictions Program is available in Malaysia.

Application requirements *Prior education:* Baccalaureate degree. *Other requirements:* college transcripts, an essay or personal statement, letter(s) of recommendation, work experience.

Completion requirements 48 semester hours are required. *Maximum time for completion:* three years.

On-campus requirements Intensive seminars on campus in Kuala Lumpur are supplemented by Internet instruction throughout the program.

INDIVIDUAL COURSE SUBJECT AREAS

Graduate
Accounting; Finance; Human Resources; International Business; Management Information Systems; Manufacturing Management; Marketing; Strategic Management

UNIVERSITY OF NEBRASKA–LINCOLN

College of Business Administration
Lincoln, Nebraska

University of Nebraska–Lincoln, founded in 1869, is a state-supported university. It is accredited by the North Central Association of Colleges and Schools.

Course delivery sites Courses are delivered to your workplace.

Media Courses are delivered via television, interactive television. Students and teachers may interact via mail, telephone, fax, e-mail, World Wide Web.

Geographic service area/restrictions Programs are available statewide.

Services Distance learners have access to library services, the campus computer network, e-mail services, academic advising at a distance.

Credit-earning options Students may transfer credits from another institution.

Typical costs Tuition of $219 per credit hour.

Registration Students may register by mail, fax, phone, e-mail, World Wide Web.

Contact Graduate Advising, University of Nebraska–Lincoln, College of Business Administration 126, Lincoln, NE 68588-0405. *Telephone:* 402-472-2338. *Fax:* 402-472-5180. *E-mail:* gradadv@cbamail.unl.edu. *Web site:* http://www.unl.edu/conted/telecom/index.html.

DEGREE & CERTIFICATE PROGRAMS

Master of Business Administration (MBA)

Application requirements *Prior education:* Baccalaureate degree. *Other requirements:* GMAT, college transcripts, letter(s) of recommendation, an application fee of $35.

Completion requirements 48 credit hours are required. *Maximum time for completion:* six years.

UNIVERSITY OF NEW ORLEANS

College of Business
New Orleans, Louisiana

University of New Orleans, founded in 1958, is a state-supported university. It is accredited by the Southern Association of Colleges and Schools.

Course delivery sites Students can receive instruction anywhere.

Media Courses are delivered via e-mail, print. Students and teachers may meet in person or interact via mail, telephone, fax, e-mail, World Wide Web.

Geographic service area/ restrictions Programs are available nationwide.

Services Distance learners have access to library services, the campus computer network, e-mail services, academic advising, tutoring, career placement assistance, bookstore at a distance.

Typical costs Tuition of $373 per course for in-state residents. Tuition of $1423 per course for out-of-state residents. *Non-credit courses:* same as the credit rate. Financial aid is available to distance learners.

Registration Students may register by mail, fax, phone.

Contact Dr. Paul J. Hensel, Associate Dean and MBA Program Director, University of New Orleans, Room BA-273, Business Building, New Orleans, LA 70148-1520. *Telephone:* 504-280-6393. *Fax:* 504-280-6958. *E-mail:* pjhmk@uno.edu. *Web site:* http://www.uno.edu.

INDIVIDUAL COURSE SUBJECT AREAS

Graduate
Finance; Marketing

UNIVERSITY OF NEW SOUTH WALES

Australian Graduate School of Management—
Executive MBA Unit
Kensington, Australia

University of New South Wales is a university in Australia.

Course delivery sites Students can receive instruction anywhere.

Media Courses are delivered via audioconferencing, computer software, World Wide Web, e-mail. Students and teachers may interact via audioconferencing, telephone, fax, e-mail, World Wide Web. The following equipment may be required: a computer with access to the Internet, a modem, and Lotus.

Geographic service area/restrictions Programs are available worldwide. Students must have at least two years of work experience and an undergraduate degree.

Services Distance learners have access to library services, the campus computer network, e-mail services, academic advising, tutoring, career placement assistance at a distance.

Credit-earning options Students may earn credits through examinations.

Typical costs Contact school for information.

Registration Students may register by mail, fax, World Wide Web.

Contact Marketing Services, University of New South Wales, Australian Graduate School of Management, Sydney, NSW 2052, Australia. *Telephone:* 0299319412. *Fax:* 0299319206. *E-mail:* carolynp@ agsm.unsw.edu.au. *Web site:* http://www.agsm.unsw.edu.au.

DEGREE & CERTIFICATE PROGRAMS

Executive Master of Business Administration (EMBA)

Application requirements *Prior education:* an undergraduate degree with five years of managerial experience. *Other requirements:* college transcripts, letter(s) of recommendation, work experience.

Change Management Qualification (CMQ)

Application requirements *Prior education:* an undergraduate degree with five years of managerial experience. *Other requirements:* college transcripts, letter(s) of recommendation, work experience.

Graduate Diploma in Management

Application requirements *Prior education:* an undergraduate degree with five years of managerial experience. *Other requirements:* college transcripts, letter(s) of recommendation, work experience.

Graduate Management Qualification (GMQ)

Application requirements *Prior education:* an undergraduate degree with five years of managerial experience. *Other requirements:* college transcripts, letter(s) of recommendation, work experience.

INDIVIDUAL COURSE SUBJECT AREAS

Graduate
Accounting; Finance; Human Resources; Information Management; Management; Marketing; Strategic Management

UNIVERSITY OF NORTH DAKOTA

College of Business and Public Administration
Grand Forks, North Dakota

University of North Dakota, founded in 1883, is a state-supported university. It is accredited by the North Central Association of Colleges and Schools. The College of Business and Public Administration first offered graduate business distance learning courses in 1991. In 1997–98, it offered 4 graduate business courses at a distance. In the fall of 1997, there were 33 students enrolled in distance learning graduate-level business courses and programs.

Course delivery sites Courses are delivered to Bismarck State College (Bismarck), Dickinson State University (Dickinson).

Media Courses are delivered via videotapes, interactive television, e-mail. Students and teachers may meet in person or interact via mail, telephone, fax, e-mail, interactive television.

Geographic service area/ restrictions Programs are available statewide. Students must be admitted to the MBA program.

Services Distance learners have access to library services, the campus computer network, e-mail services, academic advising, career placement assistance, bookstore at a distance.

Credit-earning options Students may transfer credits from another institution.

Typical costs Tuition of $1443.50 per semester for in-state residents. Tuition of $2055.50 per semester for out-of-state residents. Costs may vary by number of credits taken. Financial aid is available to distance learners.

Registration Students may register by mail, fax.

Contact Jacob Wambsganes, Professor and MBA Director, University of North Dakota, Box 8098, Grand Forks, ND 58202-8098. *Telephone:* 701-777-2975. *Fax:* 701-777-2019. *E-mail:* wambsgan@badlands.nodak. edu. *Web site:* http://www.und.nodak. edu.

DEGREE & CERTIFICATE PROGRAMS

Master of Business Administration (MBA)

In the fall of 1997 there were 33 students enrolled in this program. In 1996–97, 4 degrees were earned at a distance through this program.

Application requirements *Prior education:* Baccalaureate degree. *Other requirements:* GMAT, college transcripts, an essay or personal statement, letter(s) of recommendation, an application fee of $25.

Completion requirements 32 semester hours are required.

UNIVERSITY OF NOTRE DAME

Executive MBA Program

Notre Dame, Indiana

University of Notre Dame, founded in 1842, is an independent-religious Roman Catholic university. It is accredited by the North Central Association of Colleges and Schools. The Executive MBA Program first offered graduate business distance learning courses in 1997. In 1997–98, it offered 16 graduate business courses at a distance. In the fall of 1997, there were 6 students enrolled in distance learning graduate-level business courses and programs.

Course delivery sites Courses are delivered to 4 off-campus centers in Indianapolis, Hoffman Estates (IL), Toledo (OH).

Media Courses are delivered via videoconferencing. Students and teachers may meet in person or interact via videoconferencing, mail, telephone, e-mail.

Geographic service area/ restrictions Programs are available nationwide. Students must attend one of the receive sites. Potential students must have an undergraduate degree or an acceptable GMAT score and five years of managerial experience.

Services Distance learners have access to library services, the campus computer network, e-mail services at a distance.

Typical costs Tuition of $21,500 per year plus mandatory fees of $3400 per year. Financial aid is available to distance learners.

Contact Dr. Barry Van Dyck, Associate Director, University of Notre Dame, Executive Programs, 126 College of Business Administration, Notre Dame, IN 46556-5646. *Telephone:* 219-631-5285. *Fax:* 219-631-6783. *E-mail:* barry.vandyck.1@nd.edu.

DEGREE & CERTIFICATE PROGRAMS

Executive Master of Business Administration (EMBA)

In the fall of 1997 there were 6 students enrolled in this program. In 1996–97, 6 degrees were earned at a distance through this program.

Geographic service area/restrictions Students must attend one of the receive sites.

Application requirements *Prior education:* undergraduate degree or an acceptable GMAT score. *Other requirements:* college transcripts, an essay or personal statement, an application fee of $50, work experience, five years of managerial experience.

Completion requirements 48 credit hours are required. *Maximum time for completion:* 21 months.

On-campus requirements Students must attend campus for six days at the beginning of the fall semester plus another weekend at the start of the spring semester.

UNIVERSITY OF PHOENIX

University of Phoenix Online Campus—Center for Distance Education
Phoenix, Arizona

University of Phoenix, founded in 1976, is a proprietary comprehensive institution. It is accredited by the North Central Association of Colleges and Schools. The Center for Distance Education first offered graduate business distance learning courses in 1989. In 1997–98, it offered 80 graduate business courses at a distance. In the fall of 1997, there were 2,057 students enrolled in distance learning graduate-level business courses and programs.

Course delivery sites Students can receive instruction anywhere.

Media Courses are delivered via computer conferencing, e-mail, print. Students and teachers may meet in person or interact via mail, telephone, fax, e-mail. The following equipment may be required: a computer with a modem for online courses.

Geographic service area/restrictions Programs are available worldwide. Students must be at least 23 years old and currently employed with at least two years of work experience.

Services Distance learners have access to library services, e-mail services, academic advising at a distance.

Credit-earning options Students may transfer credits from another institution or may earn credits through examinations.

Typical costs Tuition of $5712 per year. Costs may vary by campus or location, specific program of study.

Registration Students may register by mail, fax.

Contact Center for Distance Education, University of Phoenix, 4615 East Elwood, Phoenix, AZ 85040. *Telephone:* 602-921-8014. *Fax:* 602-894-2152. *Web site:* http://www.uophx.edu.

DEGREE & CERTIFICATE PROGRAMS

Master of Arts in Organizational Management (MAOM)

Application requirements *Prior education:* Baccalaureate degree. *Other requirements:* college transcripts, an application fee of $50, work experience.

Completion requirements 41–51 credits. *Maximum time for completion:* five years.

Master of Business Administration (MBA)

Application requirements *Prior education:* Baccalaureate degree. *Other requirements:* college transcripts, an application fee of $50, work experience.

Completion requirements 41–51 credits. *Maximum time for completion:* five years.

Master of Business Administration—Global Management (MBA/GM)

Application requirements *Prior education:* Baccalaureate degree. *Other requirements:* college transcripts, an application fee of $50, work experience.

Completion requirements 41–51 credits. *Maximum time for completion:* five years.

Master of Business Administration—Technology Management (MBA/TM)

Application requirements *Prior education:* Baccalaureate degree. *Other requirements:* college transcripts, an application fee of $50, work experience.

Completion requirements 41–51 credits. *Maximum time for completion:* five years.

INDIVIDUAL COURSE SUBJECT AREAS

Graduate
Accounting; Business Communications; Business Ethics; Business Information Science; Business Law; Business Policy/Strategy; Economics; Finance; Human Resources; Information Management; International Business; International Management; Management; Marketing; Public Relations

UNIVERSITY OF PITTSBURGH

Center for Executive Education–Katz Graduate School of Business

Pittsburgh, Pennsylvania

University of Pittsburgh, founded in 1787, is a state-related university. It is accredited by the Middle States Association of Colleges and Schools. The Center for Executive Education first offered graduate business distance learning courses in 1991. In 1997–98, it offered 18 graduate business courses at a distance. In the fall of 1997, there were 39 students enrolled in distance learning graduate-level business courses and programs.

Course delivery sites Students can receive instruction anywhere.

Media Courses are delivered via audiotapes, computer software, World Wide Web, e-mail, print. Students and teachers may meet in person or interact via telephone, fax, e-mail, World Wide Web. The following equipment may be required: a computer.

Geographic service area/restrictions Programs are available worldwide. Students must have five years of business experience, college-level calculus or the equivalent, and GMAT and TOEFL (if international) scores.

Services Distance learners have access to library services, the campus computer network, e-mail services, tutoring at a distance.

Credit-earning options Students may transfer credits from another institution or may earn credits through examinations.

Typical costs Tuition of $6000 per semester. Financial aid is available to distance learners.

Registration Students may register by mail, fax.

Contact Mark T. Carter, Director, University of Pittsburgh, 301 Mervis Hall, Pittsburgh, PA 15260. *Telephone:* 412-624-4542. *Fax:* 412-648-1787. *E-mail:* mcarter@katz.business.pitt. edu. *Web site:* http://www.pitt.edu/ ~business.

DEGREE & CERTIFICATE PROGRAMS

Master of Business Administration (MBA)

In the fall of 1997 there were 39 students enrolled in this program. In 1996–97, 17 degrees were earned at a distance through this program.

Application requirements *Prior education:* Baccalaureate degree. *Other requirements:* GMAT, TOEFL (for international applicants), college transcripts, an essay or personal statement, letter(s) of recommendation, an application fee of $10, work experience, college-level calculus or the equivalent.

Completion requirements 51 credits are required. *Maximum time for completion:* two years.

On-campus requirements Students must complete 13 weeks on campus in one- to two-week units over 21 months.

UNIVERSITY OF ST. FRANCIS

College of Graduate Studies
Joliet, Illinois

University of St. Francis, founded in 1920, is an independent-religious Roman Catholic comprehensive institution. It is accredited by the North Central Association of Colleges and Schools. The College of Graduate Studies first offered graduate business distance learning courses in 1996. In 1997–98, it offered 3 graduate business courses at a distance. In the fall of 1997, there were 10 students enrolled in distance learning graduate-level business courses and programs.

Course delivery sites Students can receive instruction anywhere.

Media Courses are delivered via World Wide Web. Students and teachers may meet in person or interact via audioconferencing, mail, telephone, fax, e-mail, World Wide Web. The following equipment may be required: a computer with access to the Internet.

Geographic service area/restrictions Programs are available nationwide. The program requires admission to the appropriate graduate program.

Services Distance learners have access to library services, academic advising, bookstore at a distance.

Credit-earning options Students may transfer credits from another institution.

Typical costs Tuition of $377 per credit.

Registration Students may register by mail, fax.

Contact Dr. Joy Thompson, Associate Dean, College of Graduate Studies, University of St. Francis, 500 Wilcox Street, Joliet, IL 60435. *Telephone:* 800-735-4723. *Fax:* 815-740-3537. *E-mail:* jthompson@ stfrancis.edu. *Web site:* http://www. stfrancis.edu.

INDIVIDUAL COURSE SUBJECT AREAS

Graduate

Management; Marketing; Research and Development Administration

UNIVERSITY OF ST. THOMAS

Graduate School of Business

St. Paul, Minnesota

University of St. Thomas, founded in 1885, is an independent-religious Roman Catholic university. It is accredited by the North Central Association of Colleges and Schools. The Graduate School of Business first offered graduate business distance learning courses in 1993. In 1997–98, it offered 28 graduate business courses at a distance. In the fall of 1997, there were 105 students enrolled in distance learning graduate-level business courses and programs.

Course delivery sites Students can receive instruction anywhere.

Media Courses are delivered via computer software, computer conferencing, World Wide Web, e-mail, print. Students and teachers may meet in person or interact via mail, telephone, fax, e-mail, World Wide Web. The following equipment may be required: a computer with a modem and the appropriate software.

Geographic service area/ restrictions Programs are available nationwide. Students must be admitted into the MBA in Medical Group Management program.

Services Distance learners have access to library services, the campus computer network, e-mail services, academic advising, career placement assistance, bookstore at a distance.

Typical costs Tuition of $394 per credit. Financial aid is available to distance learners.

Registration Students may register by mail, fax, phone, e-mail, World Wide Web.

Contact Tom Gilliam, Director, MBA in Medical Group Management Program, University of St. Thomas, 1000 LaSalle Avenue, MPL 100, Minneapolis, MN 55403. *Telephone:* 612-462-4135. *Fax:* 612-962-4410. *E-mail:* shagel@stthomas.edu. *Web site:* http://www.stthomas.edu.

DEGREE & CERTIFICATE PROGRAMS

Master of Business Administration (MBA)

In the fall of 1997 there were 105 students enrolled in this program.

University of St. Thomas

In 1996–97, 30 degrees were earned at a distance through this program.

Application requirements *Prior education:* Baccalaureate degree. *Other requirements:* GMAT, college transcripts, an essay or personal statement, letter(s) of recommendation, an application fee of $30, resume, two years work experience.

Completion requirements 50 semester credits are required. *Other requirements:* students participate in the program as part of a cohort group. *Maximum time for completion:* 35 months.

On-campus requirements Students must attend campus for two one-week sessions per year.

UNIVERSITY OF SAN FRANCISCO

McLaren School of Business
San Francisco, California

University of San Francisco, founded in 1855, is an independent-religious Roman Catholic (Jesuit) university. It is accredited by the Western Association of Schools and Colleges, Inc. The McLaren School of Business first offered graduate business distance learning courses in 1990. In 1997–98, it offered 10 graduate business courses at a distance. In the fall of 1997, there were 72 students enrolled in distance learning graduate-level business courses and programs.

Course delivery sites Courses are delivered to your workplace.

Media Courses are delivered via videotapes, audiotapes, computer software, computer conferencing, World Wide Web, e-mail, print. Students and teachers may meet in person or interact via audioconferencing, mail, telephone, fax, e-mail, World Wide Web. The following equipment may be required: a TV and a VCR, a fax machine, a telephone, and/or a computer with access to the Internet and email.

Geographic service area/restrictions Programs are available worldwide. Students must be employees of corporate partners.

Services Distance learners have access to the campus computer network, e-mail services, academic advising, tutoring at a distance.

Credit-earning options Students may earn credits through examinations.

Typical costs Tuition is paid by the student's employer.

Contact University of San Francisco, *Web site:* http://www.usfca.edu/mclaren.

DEGREE & CERTIFICATE PROGRAMS

Master of Business Administration (MBA)

In the fall of 1997 there were 72 students enrolled in this program. In 1996–97, 25 degrees were earned at a distance through this program.

Geographic service area/restrictions Students must be employees of contract clients.

Application requirements *Prior education:* Baccalaureate degree. *Other requirements:* GMAT, TOEFL (for international applicants), college transcripts, an essay or personal statement, work experience, employer's endorsement and financial support.

Completion requirements 48 semester units. *Maximum time for completion:* two years.

On-campus requirements Students must be on campus for capstone courses.

UNIVERSITY OF SARASOTA

College of Business Administration
Sarasota, Florida

University of Sarasota is an independent-nonprofit graduate institution. It is accredited by the Southern Association of Colleges and Schools. The College of Business Administration first offered graduate business distance learning courses in 1992. In 1997–98, it offered 85 graduate business courses at a distance.

Course delivery sites Students can receive instruction anywhere.

Media Courses are delivered via computer software, computer conferencing, World Wide Web, e-mail, print. Students and teachers may meet in person or interact via mail, telephone, fax, e-mail, World Wide Web. The following equipment may be required: a computer with access to the Internet, email, and MS Office.

Geographic service area/ restrictions Programs are available worldwide. Applicants must be admitted as degree-seeking or at-large students.

Services Distance learners have access to library services, the campus computer network, e-mail services, academic advising, tutoring, bookstore at a distance.

Credit-earning options Students may transfer credits from another institution or may earn credits through military training.

Typical costs Tuition of $353 per semester hour plus mandatory fees of $11 per course. Costs may vary by specific program of study, number of credits taken, course delivery options. Financial aid is available to distance learners.

Registration Students may register by mail, fax, phone, e-mail.

Contact Dr. Carol Todd, Admissions, University of Sarasota, 5250 17th Street, Sarasota, FL 34235. *Telephone:* 941-379-0404. *Fax:* 991-379-9464. *E-mail:* 71722.2373@ compuserve.com. *Web site:* http:// www.sarasota.edu/distance.html.

DEGREE & CERTIFICATE PROGRAMS

Doctor of Business Administration (DBA)

In 1996–97, 24 degrees were earned at a distance through this program.

Geographic service area/ restrictions Applicants must be admitted as degree-seeking or at-large students.

Application requirements *Prior education:* Baccalaureate degree in business. *Other requirements:* college transcripts, an essay or personal statement, letter(s) of recommendation, an application fee of $50.

Completion requirements 60 semester hours are required. *Other requirements:* students must complete a comprehensive exam and a dissertation. *Maximum time for completion:* seven years.

On-campus requirements Approximately one-half of courses are completed with a short intensive residence period on campus.

Master of Business Administration (MBA)

In 1996–97, 24 degrees were earned at a distance through this program.

Geographic service area/ restrictions Applicants must be admitted as degree-seeking or at-large students.

Application requirements *Prior education:* Baccalaureate degree in business. *Other requirements:* college transcripts, an essay or personal statement, letter(s) of recommendation, an application fee of $50.

Completion requirements 36 semester hours are required. *Maximum time for completion:* four years.

On-campus requirements Approximately one-half of courses are completed with a short intensive residence period on campus.

INDIVIDUAL COURSE SUBJECT AREAS

Graduate
Finance; Human Resources; International Business; International Trade; Management; Management Information Systems; Marketing

UNIVERSITY OF SOUTH CAROLINA

College of Business Administration–MBA Office

Columbia, South Carolina

University of South Carolina, founded in 1801, is a state-supported university. It is accredited by the Southern Association of Colleges and Schools. The College of Business Administration first offered graduate business distance learning courses in 1970. In 1997–98, it offered 30 graduate business courses at a distance. In the fall of 1997, there were 325 students enrolled in distance learning graduate-level business courses and programs.

Course delivery sites Courses are delivered to your workplace, military bases, high schools, hospitals, numerous corporate receive sites, all of the University of South Carolina campuses, and all of the technical colleges in South Carolina.

Media Courses are delivered via television, interactive television. Students and teachers may meet in person or interact via audioconferencing, mail, telephone, fax, e-mail, interactive television. The following equipment may be required: access to satellite receive equipment as well as a computer with access to the Internet and email.

Geographic service area/restrictions Programs are available statewide. Students must be an admit-ted graduate student at the university as well as being able to attend some Saturday sessions on-campus.

Services Distance learners have access to e-mail services, academic advising, career placement assistance, bookstore at a distance.

Credit-earning options Students may transfer credits from another institution.

Typical costs Tuition of $185 per credit hour plus mandatory fees of $2900 per degree program for in-state residents. Tuition of $380 per credit hour plus mandatory fees of $4400 per degree program for out-of-state residents. Financial aid is available to distance learners.

Registration Students may register by phone, World Wide Web.

Contact MBA Office, University of South Carolina, College of Business Administration, Columbia, SC 29208. *Telephone:* 803-777-7940. *Fax:* 803-777-9018. *E-mail:* mba@darla.badm. sc.edu. *Web site:* http://theweb.badm. sc.edu/mba/.

DEGREE & CERTIFICATE PROGRAMS

Master of Business Administration (MBA)

In the fall of 1997 there were 320 students enrolled in this program. In 1996–97, 88 degrees were earned at a distance through this program.

Geographic service area/ restrictions Students must be an admitted graduate student at the university.

Application requirements *Prior education:* Baccalaureate degree. *Other requirements:* GMAT, college transcripts, an essay or personal statement, letter(s) of recommendation, an application fee of $35, work experience, complete application package.

Completion requirements 18 courses are required. *Maximum time for completion:* six years.

On-campus requirements Students must attend fourteen Saturday sessions per year.

UNIVERSITY OF SOUTHERN MISSISSIPPI

Graduate Business Programs
Hattiesburg, Mississippi

University of Southern Mississippi, founded in 1910, is a state-supported university. It is accredited by the Southern Association of Colleges and Schools. The Graduate Business Program first offered graduate business distance learning courses in 1997. In 1997–98, it offered 3 graduate business courses at a distance. In the fall of 1997, there were 4 students enrolled in distance learning graduate-level business courses and programs.

Course delivery sites Courses are delivered to your workplace, hospitals, specified community and junior colleges.

Media Courses are delivered via interactive television. Students and teachers may meet in person or interact via telephone, fax, e-mail. The following equipment may be required: a laptop computer with access to the Internet and specific software.

Geographic service area/restrictions Programs are available statewide.

Services Distance learners have access to library services, the campus computer network, e-mail services, career placement assistance at a distance.

Credit-earning options Students may earn credits through examinations.

Typical costs Tuition of $124 per credit hour.

Registration Students may register by phone.

Contact Dr. Ernest W. King, Director, Graduate Business Programs, University of Southern Mississippi, PO Box 5096, Hattiesburg, MS 39406. *Telephone:* 601-266-5050. *Fax:* 601-266-4639. *E-mail:* kinge@cba.usm.edu.

DEGREE & CERTIFICATE PROGRAMS

Master of Science (MS)

In the fall of 1997 there were 4 students enrolled in this program.

Application requirements *Prior education:* Baccalaureate degree. *Other requirements:* GMAT, college transcripts, an essay or personal statement, letter(s) of recommendation, work experience.

Completion requirements 32 credit hours are required. *Other requirements:* students must complete a research project. *Maximum time for completion:* six years.

INDIVIDUAL COURSE SUBJECT AREAS

Graduate
Business Law; Financial Information Systems; Financial Management/ Planning; Human Resources; Leadership; Management; Management Information Systems; Operations Management; Organizational Management; Production Management; Quality Management; Telecommunications Management

UNIVERSITY OF SOUTHERN QUEENSLAND

Australian Graduate School of Business–
Faculty of Business
Queensland, Australia

University of Southern Queensland is a university in Australia. The Australian Graduate School of Business first offered graduate business distance learning courses in 1989. In 1997–98, it offered 14 graduate business courses at a distance. In the fall of 1997, there were 1,403 students enrolled in distance learning graduate-level business courses and programs.

Course delivery sites Courses are delivered to your home, Thames Centre for Open Learning (Singapore, Singapore), 1 off-campus center.

Media Courses are delivered via videoconferencing, audiotapes, audioconferencing, computer software, World Wide Web, e-mail, print. Students and teachers may meet in person or interact via audioconferencing, mail, telephone, fax, e-mail, World Wide Web. The following equipment may be required: a computer with Windows 95 or better and access to the Internet.

Geographic service area/restrictions Programs are available worldwide.

Services Distance learners have access to library services, e-mail services, bookstore at a distance.

Credit-earning options Students may transfer credits from another institution.

Typical costs Australian students pay $800 per unit while international students pay $1050 per unit. Costs may vary by number of credits taken.

Contact Ms. Colleen Hartmann, Administration Officer, University of Southern Queensland, Faculty of Business, Toowoomba, QLD 4350, Australia. *Telephone:* 61-746311881. *Fax:* 61-746312811. *E-mail:* hartmann@usq.edu.au. *Web site:* http://www.usq.cdu.au.

DEGREE & CERTIFICATE PROGRAMS

Master of Business Administration (MBA)

In the fall of 1997 there were 758 students enrolled in this program.

In 1996–97, 43 degrees were earned at a distance through this program.

Application requirements *Prior education:* Baccalaureate degree. *Other requirements:* college transcripts, an essay or personal statement, letter(s) of recommendation, work experience.

Completion requirements 12 units are required. *Maximum time for completion:* four years.

INDIVIDUAL COURSE SUBJECT AREAS

Graduate

Accounting; Business Law; Environmental Economics/Management; Finance; Human Resources; Information Management; Marketing; Project Management

UNIVERSITY OF STRATHCLYDE

Strathclyde Graduate Business School

Glasgow, United Kingdom

University of Strathclyde is a university in the United Kingdom. The Strathclyde Graduate Business School first offered graduate business distance learning courses in 1983.

Course delivery sites Courses are delivered to your home, your workplace.

Media Courses are delivered via videotapes, audiotapes, computer software, CD-ROM, e-mail, print. Students and teachers may meet in person or interact via mail, telephone, fax, e-mail. The following equipment may be required: a computer with access to the Internet and email, access to a telephone, a fax machine, a TV and VCR, and/or an audio-casstte player.

Geographic service area/ restrictions Programs are available worldwide. Students must meet the program entrance requirements.

Services Distance learners have access to e-mail services, academic advising, tutoring at a distance.

Credit-earning options Students may earn credits through examinations, portfolio assessment.

Typical costs Tuition of $12,636 per degree program. Costs may vary by campus or location, course delivery

options. Financial aid is available to distance learners.

Contact Graduate Admissions Office, University of Strathclyde, 199 Cathedral Street, Glasgow, G4 0QU, Scotland. *Telephone:* 1415536119. *Fax:* 1415528851. *E-mail:* admissions@ sgbs.strath.ac.uk. *Web site:* http:// www.strath.ac.uk/Departments/ SGBS.

DEGREE & CERTIFICATE PROGRAMS

Master of Business Administration (MBA)

Application requirements *Prior education:* Graduate degree. *Minimum age:* 24. *Other requirements:* an essay or personal statement, letter(s) of recommendation, work experience, £200 commitment fee. Students must have GMAT scores if their degree is from a non-UK university.

Completion requirements 60 credits are required. *Maximum time for completion:* six years.

On-campus requirements Students must attend four weekend schools.

THE UNIVERSITY OF TEXAS AT DALLAS

Master of International Management Studies Program
Richardson, Texas

The University of Texas at Dallas, founded in 1969, is a state-supported university. It is accredited by the Southern Association of Colleges and Schools. The Master of International Management Studies Program first offered graduate business distance learning courses in 1996. In 1997–98, it offered 14 graduate business courses at a distance. In the fall of 1997, there were 45 students enrolled in distance learning graduate-level business courses and programs.

Course delivery sites Students can receive instruction anywhere.

Media Courses are delivered via videoconferencing, audiotapes, audioconferencing, computer software, CD-ROM, computer conferencing, World Wide Web, e-mail, print. Students and teachers may meet in person or interact via videoconferencing, audioconferencing, mail, telephone, fax, e-mail, World Wide Web. The following equipment may be required: a multimedia computer with a modem and access to the Internet.

Geographic service area/restrictions Programs are available worldwide.

Services Distance learners have access to library services, the campus computer network, e-mail services, academic advising, career placement assistance, bookstore at a distance.

Credit-earning options Students may transfer credits from another institution or may earn credits through examinations.

Typical costs Tuition of $750 per credit hour. Financial aid is available to distance learners.

Registration Students may register by mail, phone, World Wide Web.

Contact Stephen Guisinger, Professor, The University of Texas at Dallas, Box 830688—LF16, Richardson, TX 75083-0688. *Telephone:* 972-883-2715. *Fax:* 972-883-6164. *E-mail:* steveg@utdallas.edu. *Web site:* http://mimsserver.utdallas.edu/mimshome/frame.html.

DEGREE & CERTIFICATE PROGRAMS

Master of Arts (MA)

Application requirements *Prior education:* Baccalaureate degree. *Other requirements:* college transcripts, an essay or personal statement, letter(s) of recommendation, an application fee of $25, work experience, phone interview.

Completion requirements 36 credit hours are required. *Maximum time for completion:* six years.

On-campus requirements Students must be on campus for four two-day sessions.

Master of Business Administration (MBA)

Application requirements *Prior education:* Baccalaureate degree. *Other requirements:* college transcripts, an essay or personal statement, letter(s) of recommendation, an application fee of $25, work experience, phone interview.

Completion requirements 48 credit hours are required. *Maximum time for completion:* six years.

On-campus requirements Students must be on campus for four two-day sessions.

THE UNIVERSITY OF WESTERN ONTARIO

Richard Ivey School of Business
London, Ontario, Canada

The University of Western Ontario, founded in 1878, is a province-supported university. It is accredited by the American Psychological Association. The Richard Ivey School of Business first offered graduate business distance learning courses in 1995. In 1997–98, it offered 22 graduate business courses at a distance. In the fall of 1997, there were 37 students enrolled in distance learning graduate-level business courses and programs.

Course delivery sites Courses are delivered to 7 off-campus centers in London, Markham, Ottawa, Calgary (AB), Edmonton (AB), Montreal (PQ), Vancouver (BC).

Media Courses are delivered via videoconferencing. Students and teachers may meet in person or interact via videoconferencing, mail, telephone, fax, e-mail, interactive television, World Wide Web. The following equipment may be required: a computer with a modem.

Geographic service area/ restrictions Programs are available nationwide. Students must have a minimum of eight years of business experience (usually at least three years in a managerial position), acceptable GMAT scores, and meet the university degree or other educational qualifications.

Services Distance learners have access to library services, the campus computer network, e-mail services, academic advising, tutoring, career placement assistance, bookstore, Information Technology Help Desk at a distance.

Credit-earning options Students may earn credits through examinations.

Typical costs Tuition of $28,500 per degree program. Tuition is in Canadian dollars.

Contact Prof. Terry Deutscher, VEMBA Program Director, The University of Western Ontario, Ivey Business School, The University of Western Ontario, London, ON N6A 3K7, Canada. *Telephone:* 519-661-3277. *Fax:* 519-850-2341. *E-mail:* tdeutsch@ivey.uwo.ca. *Web site:* http://www.ivey.uwo.ca.

DEGREE & CERTIFICATE PROGRAMS

Master of Business Administration (MBA)

In the fall of 1997 there were 57 students enrolled in this program. In 1996–97, 36 degrees were earned at a distance through this program.

Application requirements *Prior education:* a university degree and/or work-related education. *Other requirements:* GMAT, an essay or personal statement, letter(s) of recommendation, an application fee of $200, work experience, company endorsement, a minimum of eight years business experience (usually at least three years in a managerial position).

Completion requirements 22 credits are required. *Maximum time for completion:* two years.

On-campus requirements Students must attend four one-week residence sessions and on-site classes.

UNIVERSITY OF WISCONSIN–OSHKOSH

College of Business
Oshkosh, Wisconsin

University of Wisconsin–Oshkosh, founded in 1871, is a state-supported comprehensive institution. It is accredited by the North Central Association of Colleges and Schools. The College of Business first offered graduate business distance learning courses in 1995. In 1997–98, it offered 10 graduate business courses at a distance.

Course delivery sites Courses are delivered to your home, University of Wisconsin–Green Bay (Green Bay), University of Wisconsin–Stevens Point (Stevens Point).

Media Courses are delivered via videoconferencing, interactive television, World Wide Web. Students and teachers may interact via videoconferencing, mail, telephone, fax, e-mail, interactive television, World Wide Web. The following equipment may be required: a Pentium computer (100 MHz or better) with access to the Internet, a sound card, a 28.8K modem, 23MB of RAM, Windows 95, and word processing and spread sheet software.

Geographic service area/ restrictions Programs are available nationwide. Students must be admitted to the MBA program.

Services Distance learners have access to library services, the campus computer network, e-mail services, academic advising, career placement assistance, bookstore at a distance.

Credit-earning options Students may transfer credits from another institution.

Typical costs Tuition of $250 per credit plus mandatory fees of $25 per credit for in-state residents. Tuition of $750 per credit plus mandatory fees of $25 per credit for out-of-state residents. Costs may vary by term of enrollment. Financial aid is available to distance learners.

Registration Students may register by mail, fax, phone, e-mail, World Wide Web.

Contact Lynn Grancorbitz, Assistant Director and Advisor, University of Wisconsin–Oshkosh, MBA Program, Oshkosh, WI 54901. *Telephone:* 800-633-1430. *Fax:* 920-424-7413. *E-mail:*

grancorb@uwosh.edu. *Web site:* http://www.uwosh.edu/colleges/coba/mba.htm.

DEGREE & CERTIFICATE PROGRAMS

Master of Business Administration (MBA)

Application requirements *Prior education:* Baccalaureate degree. *Other*

requirements: GMAT, college transcripts, an essay or personal statement, an application fee of $45, application form (no charge).

Completion requirements 30–51 semester hours. *Maximum time for completion:* seven years.

On-campus requirements Some courses require one to two on-campus meetings.

UNIVERSITY OF WISCONSIN– WHITEWATER

College of Business and Economics–Graduate Business Program
Whitewater, Wisconsin

University of Wisconsin–Whitewater, founded in 1868, is a state-supported comprehensive institution. It is accredited by the North Central Association of Colleges and Schools. The College of Business and Economics first offered graduate business distance learning courses in 1997. In 1997–98, it offered 8 graduate business courses at a distance.

Course delivery sites Students can receive instruction anywhere.

Media Courses are delivered via audiotapes, CD-ROM, World Wide Web, e-mail, print. Students and teachers may meet in person or interact via mail, telephone, fax, e-mail, World Wide Web. The following equipment may be required: a computer with a Pentium processor, 32MB RAM, a 28.8K modem, a CD-ROM drive, 124MB available space on the hard drive, Windows 95, and access to the Internet.

Geographic service area/restrictions Programs are available worldwide. Students must be admitted into the degree program.

Services Distance learners have access to library services, the campus computer network, e-mail services,

academic advising, career placement assistance at a distance.

Credit-earning options Students may transfer credits from another institution or may earn credits through examinations.

Typical costs Tuition of $656 per course for in-state residents. Tuition of $1856 per course for out-of-state residents. Costs may vary by number of credits taken. Financial aid is available to distance learners.

Registration Students may register by mail, fax, phone.

Contact JoAnn Oravec, Assistant Professor, University of Wisconsin– Whitewater, Carlson Hall, BEOS, Whitewater, WI 53190. *Telephone:* 414-472-5578. *Fax:* 414-472-4863. *Web site:* http://www.uww.edu.

DEGREE & CERTIFICATE
PROGRAMS

Master of Business Administration (MBA)

Application requirements *Prior education:* Baccalaureate degree in business. *Other requirements:* GMAT, TOEFL (for international applicants), college transcripts, an application fee of $45.

Completion requirements 36 credits are required. *Maximum time for completion:* seven years.

UNIVERSITY OF WYOMING

MBA Program

Laramie, Wyoming

University of Wyoming, founded in 1886, is a state-supported university. It is accredited by the North Central Association of Colleges and Schools. The MBA Program first offered graduate business distance learning courses in 1993. In 1997–98, it offered 12 graduate business courses at a distance. In the fall of 1997, there were 44 students enrolled in distance learning graduate-level business courses and programs.

Course delivery sites Courses are delivered to 13 off-campus centers in Casper, Cheyenne, Gillette, Green River, Jackson, Lander, Laramie, Powell, Rawlins, Riverton, Rock Springs, Sheridan, Torrington.

Media Courses are delivered via videoconferencing. Students and teachers may interact via mail, telephone, e-mail, interactive television, World Wide Web.

Geographic service area/restrictions Programs are available statewide. Students must be admitted to the MBA program.

Services Distance learners have access to library services, the campus computer network, e-mail services, academic advising at a distance.

Credit-earning options Students may transfer credits from another institution.

Typical costs Tuition of $193.50 per credit.

Registration Students may register by phone.

Contact MBA Office, University of Wyoming, College of Business, Laramie, WY 82071-3275. *Telephone:* 307-766-2449. *Fax:* 307-766-4028. *E-mail:* mba@uwyo.edu. *Web site:* http://www.uwyo.edu/bu/mba/mba.htm.

DEGREE & CERTIFICATE PROGRAMS

Master of Business Administration (MBA)

In the fall of 1997 there were 44 students enrolled in this program. In 1996–97, 15 degrees were earned at a distance through this program.

Application requirements *Prior education:* Baccalaureate degree. *Other*

requirements: GMAT, college transcripts, an essay or personal statement, letter(s) of recommendation.

Completion requirements 54 credit hours are required. *Other require-* *ments:* the program requires students to complete a thesis or a thesis alternative. *Maximum time for completion:* six years.

WESTERN CAROLINA UNIVERSITY

Graduate Programs in Business
Cullowhee, North Carolina

Western Carolina University, founded in 1889, is a state-supported comprehensive institution. It is accredited by the Southern Association of Colleges and Schools. The Graduate Programs in Business first offered graduate business distance learning courses in 1998. In 1997–98, it offered 5 graduate business courses at a distance.

Course delivery sites Students can receive instruction anywhere.

Media Courses are delivered via videoconferencing, computer software, computer conferencing, World Wide Web, e-mail, print. Students and teachers may meet in person or interact via videoconferencing, telephone, e-mail, interactive television, World Wide Web. The following equipment may be required: a networkable computer with the appropriate software and configuration.

Geographic service area/restrictions Programs are available worldwide. Students must be fully admitted to graduate study in business.

Services Distance learners have access to library services, the campus computer network, e-mail services, academic advising, career placement assistance, bookstore at a distance.

Typical costs Tuition of $225 per semester hour for in-state residents. Tuition of $510 per semester hour for out-of-state residents. Financial aid is available to distance learners.

Registration Students may register by mail, fax, phone, e-mail, World Wide Web.

Contact Gary A. Williams, Director, Graduate Programs in Business, Western Carolina University, Forsyth Building, Cullowhee, NC 28723. *Telephone:* 828-227-7401. *Fax:* 828-227-7414. *E-mail:* gwilliams@wcu. edu. *Web site:* http://www.wcu.edu/ cob/gradprograms/.

DEGREE & CERTIFICATE PROGRAMS

Master of Project Management (MPM)

Geographic service area/restrictions Students must be fully admitted to graduate study in business.

Application requirements *Prior education:* Baccalaureate degree. *Other requirements:* GMAT, college transcripts, letter(s) of recommendation, an application fee of $35, work experience, resume, six semester hours of prerequisites.

Completion requirements 36 semester hours are required. *Maximum time for completion:* two years.

WESTERN ILLINOIS UNIVERSITY

College of Business and Technology
Macomb, Illinois

Western Illinois University, founded in 1899, is a state-supported comprehensive institution. It is accredited by the North Central Association of Colleges and Schools. The College of Business and Technology first offered graduate business distance learning courses in 1996. In 1997–98, it offered 10 graduate business courses at a distance. In the fall of 1997, there were 32 students enrolled in distance learning graduate-level business courses and programs.

Course delivery sites Courses are delivered to 5 off-campus centers in Dixon, Freeport, Galesburg, Moline, Quincy.

Media Courses are delivered via televison, interactive television. Students and teachers may interact via mail, telephone, fax, e-mail, World Wide Web.

Geographic service area/restrictions Programs are available locally. Students must be admitted to the MBA program.

Typical costs Tuition of $93 per hour plus mandatory fees of $31.90 per hour for in-state residents. Tuition of $279 per hour plus mandatory fees of $31.90 per hour for out-of-state residents. Students must also pay an additional access fee for each course. Costs may vary by number of credits taken. Financial aid is available to distance learners.

Registration Students may register by mail, fax, phone, e-mail.

Contact Dr. David J. Bloomberg, MBA Director, Western Illinois University, College of Business and Technology, Stipes Hall 101, Macomb, IL 61455. *Telephone:* 309-298-2442. *Fax:* 309-298-1039. *E-mail:* dj-bloomberg@wiu.edu. *Web site:* http://www.wiu.edu.

DEGREE & CERTIFICATE PROGRAMS

Master of Business Administration (MBA)

In the fall of 1997 there were 32 students enrolled in this program.

Application requirements *Prior education:* Baccalaureate degree. *Other*

requirements: GMAT, college transcripts.

Completion requirements 11–20 courses. *Other requirements:* students with an undergraduate degree in business-related areas need to take fewer courses. *Maximum time for completion:* six years.

WESTERN MICHIGAN UNIVERSITY

Haworth Colege of Business
Kalamazoo, Michigan

Western Michigan University, founded in 1903, is a state-supported university. It is accredited by the North Central Association of Colleges and Schools. The Haworth Colege of Business first offered graduate business distance learning courses in 1990. In 1997–98, it offered 4 graduate business courses at a distance. In the fall of 1997, there were 50 students enrolled in distance learning graduate-level business courses and programs.

Course delivery sites Courses are delivered to 5 off-campus centers in Battle Creek, Benton Harbor, Grand Rapids, Muskegon, Traverse City.

Media Courses are delivered via televison, interactive television, audiotapes. Students and teachers may meet in person or interact via telephone, fax, e-mail, interactive television.

Geographic service area/ restrictions Programs are available statewide. Students must be admitted to the MBA program.

Services Distance learners have access to library services, the campus computer network, e-mail services, academic advising, career placement assistance, bookstore at a distance. Financial aid is available to distance learners.

Registration Students may register by phone.

Contact Gail Fredericks, Assistant Director, Distance Education, Western Michigan University, Continuing Education, Ellsworth Hall, Kalamazoo, MI 49008. *Telephone:* 616-387-4195. *Fax:* 616-387-4226. *E-mail:* gail. fredericks@wmich.edu.

DEGREE & CERTIFICATE PROGRAMS

Master of Business Administration (MBA)

In the fall of 1997 there were 50 students enrolled in this program. In 1996–97, 10 degrees were earned at a distance through this program.

Application requirements *Prior education:* Baccalaureate degree. *Other*

requirements: GMAT, college transcripts, an application fee of $25.

Completion requirements 48 semester hours are required. *Maximum time for completion:* six years.

WEST TEXAS A&M UNIVERSITY

West Texas A&M University Graduate School

Canyon, Texas

West Texas A&M University, founded in 1909, is a state-supported comprehensive institution. It is accredited by the Southern Association of Colleges and Schools. The West Texas A&M University Graduate School first offered graduate business distance learning courses in 1996. In 1997–98, it offered 5 graduate business courses at a distance. In the fall of 1997, there were 90 students enrolled in distance learning graduate-level business courses and programs.

Course delivery sites Students can receive instruction anywhere.

Media Courses are delivered via World Wide Web, e-mail. Students and teachers may interact via e-mail, World Wide Web. The following equipment may be required: a computer with a modem.

Geographic service area/restrictions Programs are available statewide.

Services Distance learners have access to library services, the campus computer network, e-mail services at a distance.

Credit-earning options Students may transfer credits from another institution.

Typical costs Tuition of $130 per credit plus mandatory fees of $50.98 per credit for in-state residents. Tuition of $258 per credit plus

mandatory fees of $50.98 per credit for out-of-state residents. *Non-credit courses:* $50 per course. Costs may vary by employment by the university. Financial aid is available to distance learners.

Registration Students may register by phone.

Contact Dr. Ron Hiner, MBA Coordinator, West Texas A&M University, PO Box 60187, Canyon, TX 79016. *Telephone:* 806-651-2517. *Fax:* 806-651-2514. *E-mail:* rhiner@wtmail.wtamu.edu. *Web site:* http://www.wtamu.edu.

INDIVIDUAL COURSE SUBJECT AREAS

Graduate

Accounting; Business Communications; Business Law; Economics; Finance; Management; Management Information Systems; Marketing

WEST VIRGINIA UNIVERSITY

College of Business and Economics—Graduate Programs

Morgantown, West Virginia

West Virginia University, founded in 1867, is a state-supported university. It is accredited by the North Central Association of Colleges and Schools. In 1997–98, it offered 17 graduate business courses at a distance. In the fall of 1997, there were 220 students enrolled in distance learning graduate-level business courses and programs.

Course delivery sites Courses are delivered to Bluefield State College (Bluefield), Greenbriar Community College (Lewisburg), West Virginia Northern Community College (Wheeling), 4 off-campus centers in Beckley, Kanawha Valley, Parkersburg, Shepardstown.

Media Courses are delivered via videotapes, videoconferencing, interactive television, audioconferencing, computer software, CD-ROM, World Wide Web, e-mail, print. Students and teachers may meet in person or interact via videoconferencing, mail, telephone, fax, e-mail, World Wide Web. The following equipment may be required: a computer meeting specific software criteria.

Geographic service area/restrictions Programs are available in West Virginia and surrounding counties in Maryland, Ohio, Pennsylvania, and Virginia. Students must have two years of work experience and a baccalaureate or first degree or a baccalaureate-equivalent degree.

Services Distance learners have access to the campus computer network, e-mail services, academic advising, tutoring, career placement assistance at a distance.

Typical costs Tuition of $158 per credit for in-state residents. Tuition of $449 per credit for out-of-state residents. Financial aid is available to distance learners.

Registration Students may register by mail, fax, phone, e-mail.

Contact Candy A. Ramsey, Assistant Director, West Virginia University, College of Business and Economics, PO Box 6025, Morgantown, WV 26505. *Telephone:* 304-293-7811. *Fax:*

West Virginia University

304-293-2385. *E-mail:* cramsey2@
wvu.edu. *Web site:* http://www.wvu.
edu.

DEGREE & CERTIFICATE PROGRAMS

Executive Master of Business Administration (EMBA)

Geographic service area/ restrictions Program is available statewide.

Application requirements *Prior education:* Baccalaureate degree. *Other requirements:* GMAT, college transcripts, an application fee of $45, work experience.

Completion requirements 48 credits are required. *Maximum time for completion:* two years.

On-campus requirements Students must attend campus once per semester.

Master of Professional Accountancy (MPA)

Geographic service area/ restrictions Program is available statewide.

Application requirements *Prior education:* Baccalaureate degree. *Other requirements:* GMAT, college transcripts, an application fee of $45.

Completion requirements 48 credits are required. *Maximum time for completion:* two years.

On-campus requirements Students must attend campus once per semester.

WINTHROP UNIVERSITY
College of Business Administration
Rock Hill, South Carolina

Winthrop University, founded in 1886, is a state-supported comprehensive institution. It is accredited by the Southern Association of Colleges and Schools. In 1997–98, it offered 6 graduate business courses at a distance. In the fall of 1997, there were 35 students enrolled in distance learning graduate-level business courses and programs.

Course delivery sites Courses are delivered to Coastal Carolina University (Conway).

Media Courses are delivered via interactive television, computer software, computer conferencing, e-mail, print. Students and teachers may meet in person or interact via telephone, fax, e-mail, interactive television.

Geographic service area/restrictions Programs are available locally. Students must be admitted to the MBA program.

Services Distance learners have access to library services, the campus computer network, e-mail services, academic advising, career placement assistance, bookstore at a distance.

Credit-earning options Students may transfer credits from another institution.

Typical costs Tuition of $164 per semester hour for in-state residents. Tuition of $294 per semester hour for out-of-state residents. Costs may vary by number of credits taken. Financial aid is available to distance learners.

Registration Students may register by fax, phone, e-mail.

Contact Peggy Hager, Director of Graduate Studies, Winthrop University, College of Business Administration, Rock Hill, SC 29733. *Telephone:* 803-323-2409. *Fax:* 803-323-2539. *E-mail:* hagerp@mail. winthrop.edu.

DEGREE & CERTIFICATE PROGRAMS

Master of Business Administration (MBA)

In the fall of 1997 there were 35 students enrolled in this program. In 1996–97, 10 degrees were earned at a distance through this program.

Application requirements *Prior education:* Baccalaureate degree. *Other requirements:* GMAT, college

transcripts, an essay or personal statement, an application fee of $35.

Completion requirements 39 semester hours are required. *Maximum time for completion:* six years.

INDIVIDUAL COURSE SUBJECT AREAS

Graduate
Accounting; Business Communications; Business Policy/Strategy;

Finance; Industrial/Labor Relations; Information Management; Management; Marketing; Quantitative Analysis

WORCESTER POLYTECHNIC INSTITUTE

Graduate Management Programs
Worcester, Massachusetts

Worcester Polytechnic Institute, founded in 1865, is an independent-nonprofit university. It is accredited by the New England Association of Schools and Colleges. The Graduate Management Program first offered graduate business distance learning courses in 1979. In 1997–98, it offered 7 graduate business courses at a distance. In the fall of 1997, there were 30 students enrolled in distance learning graduate-level business courses and programs.

Course delivery sites Students can receive instruction anywhere.

Media Courses are delivered via videotapes, videoconferencing, World Wide Web. Students and teachers may meet in person or interact via videoconferencing, mail, telephone, fax, e-mail, World Wide Web. The following equipment may be required: a PC or MAC with a modem and access to the Internet and email. Students may also need access to a fax machine, a TV and a VCR, and a video camera.

Geographic service area/restrictions Programs are available worldwide. Students are required to have a baccalaureate degree.

Services Distance learners have access to library services, the campus computer network, e-mail services, academic advising, tutoring, career placement assistance, bookstore at a distance.

Credit-earning options Students may transfer credits from another institution or may earn credits through examinations.

Typical costs Tuition of $612 per credit. Costs may vary by number of credits taken, overseas shipping charges for videotapes. Financial aid is available to distance learners.

Registration Students may register by mail, fax, World Wide Web.

Contact Norman D. Wilkinson, Director, Graduate Management Programs, Worcester Polytechnic Institute, 100 Institute Road,

Worcester, MA 01609-2280. *Telephone:* 508-831-5218. *Fax:* 508-831-5720. *E-mail:* wpigmp@wpi.edu. *Web site:* http://mgnt.wpi.edu/graduate.htm.

DEGREE & CERTIFICATE PROGRAMS

Master of Business Administration (MBA)

In the fall of 1997 there were 30 students enrolled in this program. In 1996–97, 5 degrees were earned at a distance through this program.

Application requirements *Prior education:* Baccalaureate degree. *Other requirements:* GMAT, TOEFL (for international applicants), college transcripts, an essay or personal statement, letter(s) of recommendation, an application fee of $50.

Completion requirements 31–49 credits.

INDIVIDUAL COURSE SUBJECT AREAS

Graduate

Entrepreneurship; Leadership; Management Information Systems; Manufacturing Management; Marketing; Operations Management; Organizational Behavior/Development; Technology Management

WORCESTER POLYTECHNIC INSTITUTE

Graduate Management Programs

Advanced Distance Learning Network
Worcester, Massachusetts

THE INSTITUTE

Worcester Polytechnic Institute (WPI), the third-oldest private technological university in the United States, has been a pioneer in technology-based higher education since its founding in 1865. It is fully accredited by the New England Association of Schools and Colleges. WPI's mission is to educate talented men and women in preparation for careers of professional practice, civic contribution, and leadership.

The university has earned a reputation for academic excellence in technological education, practical application to the challenges of the marketplace, and a faculty of renowned academicians and industry experts who are practitioners in their fields. Most of WPI's academic departments offer master's and doctoral programs and support leading-edge research in a broad range of fields.

DISTANCE LEARNING PROGRAM

WPI offers full- and part-time graduate management study at its campuses in Worcester and Waltham, Massachusetts, as well as worldwide via its Advanced Distance Learning Network (ADLN). In response to the need for increased flexibility in part-time graduate management education, WPI supplemented its on-campus offerings with a complete Master of Business Administration (M.B.A.) via the ADLN. Through a combination of modern communication and instructional technologies, the WPI M.B.A. is available to working professionals at home or work.

WPI's M.B.A. program is a highly integrated, applications-oriented M.B.A. program. The WPI M.B.A. provides students with both the big-picture perspective required of successful upper-level managers and the hands-on knowledge needed to meet the daily demands of the workplace. WPI's focus on the management of technology comes from the recognition that rapidly changing technology is driving the pace of business. WPI ensures that its students understand leading and managing in high-technology organizations, converting technology into new products and services that the market values, and integrating technology into the workplace. The program's strong emphasis on behavioral skills prepares students to be leaders in any organization, and the global threads throughout the curriculum ensure that students understand the global imperative facing all businesses. The complete WPI

M.B.A. may be earned via distance education with no residency requirement.

DELIVERY MEDIA

The predominant method of delivery for ADLN courses is via individual videocassettes that are delivered directly to the student. Tapes are sent via express mail weekly when following the on-campus section of a course or in a single package for courses taped earlier. ADLN students fully participate in their courses via electronic means (Internet, e-mail, phone, and fax). WPI also delivers a limited number of graduate management courses on line and via videoconferencing.

ADLN students are required to have a PC or Macintosh computer and modem, an e-mail account, Internet access, and access to a fax machine, videocassette player, and video camera (not needed for all courses). Instructional and administrative support personnel are easily accessible by telephone, fax, and e-mail and are readily available to answer questions and consult on course subjects.

SPECIAL PROGRAMS

WPI also offers two highly specialized 30-credit Master of Science (M.S.) programs that are specifically designed for individuals who seek advanced academic training in a particular area. These include the M.S. in marketing and technological innovation and the M.S. in operations and information technology. All graduate management degree programs provide internship, thesis, and independent study options.

FACULTY

The Department of Management has 19 faculty members, 15 full-time and 4 part-time, of whom 18 have Ph.D.'s. In addition to teaching, Department of Management faculty members are involved in a variety of sponsored research and consulting work. A sampling of current research includes quality control in information-handling processes, supply chain management, financial distress, environmentally conscious manufacturing, international accounting differences, strategy and new venture teams, and re-engineering business education.

STUDENT SERVICES

Academic advisers are assigned upon admission. Online library services are free. Dial-up UNIX accounts (for e-mail and other applications) and career placement and counseling are available for matriculated students. Books can be ordered from the WPI bookstore (888-WPI-BOOKS, toll-free) and are typically delivered one to three days after ordering.

CREDIT OPTIONS

The M.B.A. program allows 18 foundation-level credits to be waived for those with appropriate academic backgrounds, either via straight waivers for those with appropriate course work completed within the past six years with a grade of B or better or via waiver exams. The M.B.A. program also allows the transfer of up to 9 credits from graduate-level course work completed at other schools.

ADMISSION

Admission to WPI's Graduate Management Programs is competitive. Applicants should have the analytic aptitude and academic preparation necessary to complete a technology-oriented management program. This includes a minimum of two semesters of college-level calculus or three semesters of other college-level math course work. Applicants are also required to have an understanding of computer systems.

Current students have an average GMAT score of 560 and an average undergraduate GPA of 3.1. The minimum TOEFL score requirement is 550.

TUITION AND FEES

Tuition for 1998–99 is $636 per credit hour for all graduate-level courses ($1908 per 3-credit course).

FINANCIAL AID

Loan-based aid is available to students registered for at least 6 credits per semester.

APPLYING

Applicants to the M.B.A. program must submit the program application, three letters of recommendation, official transcripts from all previously attended colleges, official GMAT scores, official TOEFL scores (international applicants only), and a $50 application fee. Admission is granted on a rolling basis. Admission decisions are made within a month of receipt of a completed application. There is no requirement for distance students to attend an on-campus orientation.

CONTACT

Norman D. Wilkinson
Director, Graduate Management
 Programs
Worcester Polytechnic Institute
100 Institute Road
Worcester, Massachusetts 01609-
 2280
Telephone: 508-831-5218
Fax: 508-831-5720
E-mail: wpigmp@wpi.edu
Web site: http://mgnt.wpi.edu

Geographic Index

MBA–Distance Learning Programs

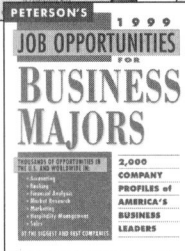